The Directors Guild of America Oral History Series

1. Byron Haskin. 1984.
2. Worthington Miner. 1985.
3. Curtis Bernhardt. 1986.
4. King Vidor. 1988.
5. David Butler. 1993.
6. Stuart Heisler.
7. Henry Koster. 1987.
8. Ira Skutch. 1989.
9. Norman Lloyd. 1990.
10. Jack, Jules, & Sam White. 1990.
11. Arthur Jacobson. 1991.
12. Andrew Marton. 1991.
13. Norman Corwin. 1994.

A Directors Guild of America Oral History

Years of the Electric Ear

NORMAN CORWIN

Interviewed by Douglas Bell

The Directors Guild of America
& The Scarecrow Press, Inc.
Metuchen, N.J., & London, 1994

British Library Cataloguing-in-Publication data available

Library of Congress Cataloging-in-Publication Data

Corwin, Norman Lewis, 1910-
    Years of the electric ear : Norman Corwin / interviewed by Douglas
Bell.
        p. cm. — (The Directors Guild of America oral history series
; 13)
        Includes bibliographical references and index.
        ISBN 0-8108-2885-5
        1. Corwin, Norman Lewis, 1910 - . 2. Radio producers and
directors—United States—Interviews. 3. Radio broadcasting—United
States—History. I. Bell, Douglas. II. Title. III. Title: Norman
Corwin. IV. Series.
        PN1991.4.C64A3 1994
        791.44 ' 0232 ' 092—dc20
        [B]   94-5101

To Charles Kuralt

Years of the Electric Ear

Years of the electric ear!
The heavens crackling with report: far-flung,
    nearby, idle, consequential
The worst of bad news and the best of good
Seizures and frenzies of opinion
The massive respirations of government and
    commerce
Sofa-sitters taken by kilocycle to the ball park,
    the concert hall, the scene of the crime
Dramas that let us dress the sets ourselves
Preachments and prizefights
The time at the tone, the weather will be, and
    now for a word
The coming of wars and freeways
Outcroppings of fragmented peace
Singing commercials and *The Messiah*.

And then the eye......

— From *Network at Fifty*
(written by Norman Corwin
for the 50th anniversary of CBS
and read on the air by Walter Cronkite)

Contents

Foreword

by Charles Champlin

Like the fortunate writers and directors who worked in live television in the late 1940s and early 1950s, Norman Corwin had found himself, hardly more than a dozen years earlier, on the ground floor (so to speak) of radio, which like live television had only begun to discover and exploit its immense creative possibilities and its matchless powers of communication.

Corwin was still a newspaperman when he first became involved with radio in 1934. The medium had been around for several years (as television had been in the 1950s), but the crystal sets and the thrill of picking up KDKA on a clear night were only yesterday, and the phenomenon of radio was a novelty that had only lately started to take form as an industry.

The joining of Corwin and radio was as timely as creative linkings ever get. He was furiously energetic, with boundless curiosity and limitless ideas, a poet and essayist, a student of history, politics, philosophy and the society he lived in, and a man with an instinctive affinity for the microphone and radio's unique gift of stimulating the imagination to paint its own pictures. Above all, Corwin was an idealist and an optimist who saw that radio could not only entertain and divert but could also move its listeners to think and feel and comprehend both the perils and the glories of their days.

The other half of the fortunate timing was that CBS, where Corwin did almost all of his significant early work, was uniquely receptive to his talent and his innovations, less concerned with size of audience than size of concept. Most of Corwin's early broadcasts were sustaining, unsponsored. Like the CBS news staff, symbolized by the presence of Edward R. Murrow, Eric Sevareid and other voices that resonate down the years, Corwin's *Columbia Workshop*, which he produced and directed from 1938, was a prestigious, class act for the network.

The remarkable radio history of Norman Corwin is chronicled in these conversations, and in the detailed chronology at the end. What is significant is that the titles of the series — including not only the *Columbia Workshop* but also *Americans at Work, Words Without Music, 26 By Corwin, This Is War, An American in England* and *Columbia Presents Corwin* have defeated the usually ephemeral nature of radio and live on, in print, reproduction and scholarly study more than a half-century after they were first broadcast. It is true as well of individual programs, from *The Plot to Overthrow Christmas* to his VE Day special, *On a Note of Triumph* (which is frequently rebroadcast), a unique acknowledgment of the event but also of the writer-director. Corwin's were pieces which helped to define what radio at its best could do, and they are part of our national cultural heritage.

Now in his eighties, Corwin remains to an extraordinary degree the man he was described as being sixty years ago — furiously energetic and creative, passionate about ideas, an acute observer of his times, a lover of the American past and most particularly the genius of the American founding fathers. His idealism remains intact, although his optimism, as he remarks in the conversations, has been dented by events, as revealed by the titles of two of the more recent of his seventeen books, *Trivializing America* and *Holes in a Stained Glass Window*.

Like the fine and humane commentator on the West, Wallace Stegner, whom he resembles as a loving but knowing and critical observer of late Twentieth Century America, Norman Corwin can be seen, and best understood, as an exemplar of a great tradition: the stalwart, fearlessly independent thinker, able to see civilization as a continuity stretching from the deep and unknowable past toward an unknowable and probably dangerous future. Neither a preacher nor a dogmatist, Corwin is, as Stegner was, a man of values, inner-directed and marching to his own drum, a true believer in Jeffersonian democracy and the inalienable rights to which each of us is born.

Given his self-effacing modesty (which however never inhibits his proclamation of the truth as he sees it), Norman Corwin may claim to be no more than a working writer and director, whose chores are far from finished. But he stands as a man of high if rumpled nobility, wonderfully and clearly revealed in these pages in all his intensity, his unsparing candor about himself and all else, his wisdom and his abiding regard for humankind, with all our frailties and follies.

Los Angeles
February 1994

Charles Champlin, Arts Editor Emeritus for the *Los Angeles Times*, is a longtime columnist and film critic, and a longtime friend of Norman Corwin. He is the author of *George Lucas: The Creative Impulse* (Abrams, 1992).

Acknowledgments

As his credits at the end of this volume attest, Norman Corwin is, in popular industry parlance, a prolific "hyphenate" — a highly respected writer-director-producer-teacher. Now in his eighties, this award-winning director and author of countless radio shows, television shows, films, plays, poems and books, currently teaches an honors class, "Specialized Reporting: The Arts," at the University of Southern California School of Journalism. Just recently, in December 1993, he completed a radio revival in Los Angeles of his acclaimed work, *The Plot to Overthrow Christmas*.

The story of his unique career, told here in his own words, is especially valuable for placing radio drama in historical context. Influential in the rise of radio as an entertainment art form (he was lovingly nicknamed the "Shakespeare of Radio"), he was also a witness to its decline. Following a prophetic conversation with CBS's William Paley on the Santa Fe *Chief* just after World War II, Corwin wrote: "The name of the doomed was Radio, my first love, still rich, still big, but in the terminal phase of the wasting disease that was to end its usefulness as a medium for any serious artist."

As part of Directors Guild of America Special Projects, headed by National Special Projects Officer Selise E. Eiseman, the DGA Oral History Program is dedicated to recording the memories of those DGA members who, as seminal figures in the development of film, television and radio, offer insight into an important segment of American cultural history. Since its inception in 1979, more than 40 oral histories have been undertaken, and have been archived in original audiotape and transcript form in the Guild's Los Angeles Robert E. Wise Library. Roughly a third have subsequently been published or are in preparation for publication, after being edited for historical accuracy, chronology, grammar and spelling.

The interviews with Norman Corwin, commissioned by David Shepard through the DGA, were conducted in 1987 by Douglas Bell at Corwin's office in West Los Angeles. Credits research, editorial restructuring into chapters, and indexing were completed by Aubrey Horton and Kevin Hindley, with proofreading assistance and factchecking by Ira Skutch, Josh Ryan, Ian Noel, and Jack DuBois. The dustjacket was designed by Andrew Hadel.

Adele Field
Oral Histories Editor
Directors Guild of America

Chapter 1

DOUGLAS BELL: You grew up in Boston. It seems to have had a striking effect on how you developed and what you subsequently chose to write about.

NORMAN CORWIN: It did. One cannot avoid being aware of the history in those parts because it's there in the nomenclature. I lived in a section of the city where the streets were named Bennington and Ticonderoga and Saratoga. I went to the James Otis Grammar School. The Bunker Hill monument was visible a short distance from my home. In the entrances and exits from the city of Boston proper to its suburbs to the north, one took a ferry very close to Tea Wharf where the tea party was staged. It was inevitable that the history be part of the atmosphere, the ambience.

BELL: Did it affect you more than others around you?

CORWIN: I don't think so. I think that my appreciation of the uniqueness of American history came later, came actually when I was in a position to digest that history and write works that reflected it. One does not have to have issued from any particular fabric in order to see the whole pattern.

BELL: Were your parents native Bostonians?

CORWIN: No, they were not, but very close to that. Both parents arrived at a very early age when they were three or four. My mother was born in Hungary, and my father was born in London; so I cannot say that they came over on the Mayflower, though those people were immigrants, too.

BELL: That was in the 1880s or 1890s?

CORWIN: Yes, I would say that my father was here by 1880.

BELL: What did he do for a living?

CORWIN: You mean as an adult? He was a printer. I ask "as an adult" not in an antic way, but because he left school and sold newspapers. His family was poor. In his late teens he became a printer, a printer in the old renaissance sense of the term in that he didn't work with high-speed machines. He worked with a hand-operated plate press on which one impression at a time was made.

BELL: Single sheet.

CORWIN: Single sheet, single card — yes. They were inked by hand. This was mostly engraving, not the kind of printing that we have today with typefaces. He worked for the Mackenzie Engraving Company which no longer exists. For a period of several decades, it was one of the leading companies of its kind in the country. He became foreman of a department, and there might have been fifteen or twenty printers under him. He trained a good many men who went on to the United States Bureau of Printing and Engraving.

BELL: You were not an only child.

CORWIN: I was born the youngest of three brothers, and I have a younger sister.

BELL: What did your brothers Emil and Alfred do for a living in later life?

CORWIN: Al was in public relations work and is now retired and living in New York. My brother Emil, the eldest brother, is still at work with the Food and Drug Administration in Washington, D.C. He writes material for them, deals with the media, and is one of the ombudsmen of the FDA.

BELL: He wasn't compelled to retire?

CORWIN: No, and he's in his eighties. This year he swears will be his last with the FDA. [Ed. note: He was still with the FDA at 91.]

BELL: You were seven years old when the United States entered World War I. Do you remember that very vividly?

CORWIN: I don't remember it as vividly as I would like, but I was aware of it. I certainly remember the newspaper headlines. I have a very clear recollection of the Armistice, dramatized for me by the fact that a woman in the tenement house in which we lived — they were called tenements in those days, not apartments — lost a son on the *U.S.S. Tampa.* I think it was a destroyer or a subchaser. It was torpedoed with all hands lost. He was a marvelous young man, and I remember how tragic that was — the circumstance of an armistice where you could not help but feel her loss, that her son did not survive.

BELL: Do you remember seeing her that day?

CORWIN: I remember hearing her cry. I did not see her, but I remember hearing her cry as I passed by her door. By the way, that young man was David Hoffman for whom a building on the campus of Harvard was named. He had two older brothers, Robert and Arnold Hoffman, who struck it rich in gold mining and presented to Harvard a mining-sciences building named for him.

BELL: Do you remember your family affairs, your family finances, very well?

CORWIN: Indeed I do. I contributed to them.

BELL: By what age?

CORWIN: About the age of ten, eleven, twelve, around there — working in my father's plant. It was really large, several floors. I worked on the night shift — from midnight to eight in the morning — in the summers. I made pretty good money for the time.

BELL: Were you a good student?

CORWIN: No, I was an indifferent student. I was good in English, and I was good in the subjects that interested me. But I was hopeless in the mathematical studies. I was shamefully inept at Algebra and Geometry, and to this day I don't understand how I got a "C" grade in them.

BELL: The end of your high school days coincided with the beginning of the Depression. Was that a contributing factor in your deciding not to go to college?

CORWIN: No, it wasn't. I finished high school in, I believe, 1926, and the Depression really hit in 1929. I lost no time moving into employment on a newspaper. To get the job, I sent out letters to eighty different papers, making a list from a directory of all the newspapers in the country. I took those that were within a 150-mile radius of Boston and wrote to them individually. I sent out eighty letters and got fifty-one replies, which was pretty good.

Of the fifty-one replies, three held out the possibility of some kind of employment in the future. They would keep my name, and if I got in touch with them in two or three months' time, they might have an opening. One of those did materialize, in a town that was about 120 miles from Boston. So I, Poor Richard, got on a train and went out to take this job.

BELL: What town was it?

CORWIN: Greenfield, Massachusetts. The *Greenfield Daily Recorder*. It was a small-town daily. The town was situated in the eastern end of the Mohawk trail, almost on the Vermont border.

BELL: What did you do on the paper?

CORWIN: Everything. I was a reporter. I became a film critic at the age of nineteen and ran a column headed, "Seeing Things in the Dark" — which I still think is a pretty good name for a movie review. It was pretty cheeky of a nineteen-year-old to sit in judgment of movies from Hollywood. After filing two or three of my reviews that were extremely negative, the proprietor of the local movie house made it known that I was *persona non grata* as a freebie and that henceforth the paper would have to pay for my seat, which they did.

BELL: Do you remember the movies?

CORWIN: No, but I remember that sound came in during that period.

BELL: Was it a one-theater town?

CORWIN: I think there were two, but this was in the era when it was obligatory on the part of movie houses to have fancy furbishings. So the ceiling was painted to resemble a sky, there were clouds; and when the lights went out, there were twinkling stars. It was very ambitious for a small town. It was the small-town version of one of those great glory houses like the Roxy or the Paramount.

BELL: Have you been back to that town recently?

CORWIN: I never returned. I left it to take a job forty miles down the Connecticut River, in the much bigger city of Springfield, Massachusetts. I believe that was in 1929.

BELL: So you were still casting about for jobs while working, or did you catch the attention of someone in Springfield?

CORWIN: I caught the attention of my brother who worked for the *Springfield Republican.* He learned of an opening there and asked me to come on down. He was about to leave to take some other job, and he recommended me to the editor, and the editor said okay.

Though it was called the *Springfield Republican*, that did not describe its politics — it was highly independent. The Bowles family, which owned it, was for a while the oldest newspaper dynasty in America. Chester Bowles went to India as an ambassador. Samuel Bowles was the originator.

This paper had a very distinguished record, and a great many important journalists worked on it before I got there. I think Brooks Atkinson was one. Perhaps Henry Luce put in some time there. Men of that caliber. For a time it was considered a kind of prep school for New York journalists.

BELL: Did you have more specific duties there than at Greenfield?

CORWIN: No, fortunately for me. But I was a good reporter, I must say for myself.

BELL: What makes a good reporter?

CORWIN: First of all, the ability to write. I wrote pretty well, well enough for them to choose me to handle the color stories and the nuts who came around with bizarre and unusual stories. Several of these pieces worked their way into national attention, originating in little Springfield with its 150,000 residents. One of these was the ash-can rolling champion of the world, a man named Carlo Tranghese who worked for the city's sanitation department. He came to the city room one day, saying that he had developed a new sport, one that should be brought to the attention of the world because it involved a new skill. The object of ash-can rolling was to take an ash can — full of ashes, you understand, not just a featherweight item — and twirl it, whirl it without spilling any ashes over a given distance. He would defy anyone in the world to do it any better than he did.

I wrote up this ringing challenge, and it appeared on the front page of the *Republican*. His challenge was answered by a man named Arthur Lisee who introduced a note of patriotic fervor in that he painted his ash can red, white, and blue. And I as a moving spirit, a Tex Rickard, set up a contest. It was a public event. We picked as our arena a public school which had a very large apron of cement around it. The race course was once around the school. There was a very big turnout, and Mr. Tranghese won with a late rally.

This was given play locally. But then the interest faded, and the inattention bothered Mr. Tranghese. So about three months later he came to me with the story that he had had a lot of wine in his cellar, barrels of it, and that it had been turned to water, which is a miracle in reverse.

"Look," I said, "that's of less interest to me than how you are wearing your crown as the world's champion ash-can roller."

"That's really the reason I came to see you," he said. "Something's got to be done. There's been no follow up."

I'm translating into English what this man said in very broken English. He was a sweet guy and didn't have much vocabulary, but he expressed what he wanted to say.

"I'll tell you what I'll do, Carlo," I said. "I'll write a letter for you to the New York State Athletic Commission asking for permission to demonstrate your art in Times Square." So I did and thought nothing about it. That was the end of it as far as I was concerned. But about a week later one of my colleagues rushed in from the wire room to say, "My God, the A.P. has got a story that the New York State Athletic Commission has received a letter requesting that the ash-can rolling champion of the world be given permission to demonstrate in Times Square!" The story went on to say that they referred the application to the sanitation department.

Anyway, all of the great newspaper columnists in the country grabbed that story and ran with it. It was covered by Beverly Smith — one of those strange unisex names like Marion — and he had a column named "The Lantern" in the New *York Herald-Tribune*. It was also covered by a famous sportswriter, who had a national readership — you will never have heard of him — named Hype Igoe, whose first name means something quite different today. And it was covered by O. O. McIntire, another writer who was famous for fifteen minutes. It was in that era.

All these men wrote columns about it. And when the local radio station became aware that this was a national story and that reports about it were coming over the wires, I suddenly became vice-president in charge of Carlo Tranghese. The radio station, WBZA, asked me if I would interview Carlo. I had never been on the air. That was unique in those days. Radio was very new, and it was still a novelty. The editors of the *Springfield Republican*, which as I've explained was no little country weekly, were interested and listened to that broadcast.

BELL: Who owned the station?

CORWIN: There were two, and they both were big Westinghouse stations — WBZ in Boston and WBZA in Springfield. They operated then, as now, in synchronization.

Now this whole set of circumstances was flukey and of small moment, but as it turned out it had big consequences for me. About six months later, WBZA came to the *Republican* and said: "We would like to do a 15-minute nightly newscast at 10:30 or 10:45 in the evening to be heard in both cities."

Boston being a major city, this was a major setup. So the _Republican_ said sure, and it was a _quid pro quo_ deal. The editors, having heard me on the air, picked me for the job. In this way I became familiar with the microphone. It became part of my background.

BELL: How long did that last?

CORWIN: A couple of years. You see, at that time they did not have the network newscasts that we have today, nothing of that kind. Radio in those days was considered an upstart by newspapers. They felt it was a competitor. They were afraid of it, and they didn't want to abet it in any way. The _Springfield Republican_ departed from that policy of non-cooperation and said yes. Of course, the station was delighted.

BELL: So they would give the _Republican_ a plug every night, or you would say "This is Norman Corwin of the _Springfield Republican_"?

CORWIN: Yes, exactly. I got no extra pay for newscasting, incidentally. That was only part of my job. I remember I used to go to the YMCA. I did modest workouts there, and I remember overhearing in the locker room, while changing to civvies after a workout, two guys who didn't know that I heard them talking about me.

One of them said, "That fellow is Corwin, the guy who's on the air." They talked about me, not in any damaging way, but speculating about what I earned. "He must make a lot of dough." That was ironic in that in the Depression my weekly salary was $32 — marked down from $35 because we went from a six-day to a five-day week. But we have to bear in mind that $32 then was not bad.

BELL: What was the state of WBZ's programming in 1930?

CORWIN: Much of it was feed. I think they were then a member of the Blue Network of NBC. They did a good deal of local programming as well. I became the radio editor of the *Springfield Republican* after a while, both the daily and Sunday paper. There were some first-class critics on the roster of that paper.

BELL: So you had a longer Sunday piece?

CORWIN: I not only had a Sunday piece but a Sunday page which was pretty generous space for radio then. I came up with ideas for dealing with radio news and, if I may say so, a form of radio listing that was ahead of its time. It had a heading similar in spirit to "Seeing Things in the Dark" — which was "Where to Find What You Want When You Want It." It listed programs by category — religious, sports, drama, music, news — which I don't think is done universally today. This classifying was very much appreciated by the editors and readers.

BELL: In 1935 you wrote in the *Republican*: "The extent of creative genius in radio can be compared to that of a convention of plasterers and plumbers."

CORWIN: That was a strange quote from me, young and brash as I was. And while there was some substance to it, it was an overstatement. I'm afraid that my judgments in that period were, to be charitable, immature. But I used my rank as radio editor to suggest gently to WBZA that they might do a program featuring me because I had an interest in poetry. I wanted to bring to the air not my own poetry but the work of the great poets.

Before I had this notion, I decided to collaborate with a man named Benjamin Kalman, a very good pianist. I thought it would be nice if we got together on such a program — but not in any way to set the music behind the poetry in importance, which would do a disservice to both the music and the poetry. Without making a fuss or going into musicological ramifications or being longhaired about it, I simply read each poem; and we followed it with music that more or less conveyed the spirit of the writing. It was not done in a formal way, "And now we shall hear the second movement of Chopin's sonata in C minor." We just went right into it. I talked briefly about the poems and their authors and gave a little background before I spoke the pieces.

So the Tranghese episode got me the radio job, which got me the radio editorship, which got me the radio program, which by the way, we called *Rhymes and Cadences*. That name sounds pretty simplistic, but it served its purpose. It was the precursor of the first program that I did of a proprietary nature, *Words Without Music*, which I produced for CBS.

BELL: What were your real objections to the general run of programming at that time as a radio editor?

CORWIN: I was not a rager against radio as I had been with movies. Bear in mind that the incidence of program trash, as compared to the total programming of American radio, was far smaller than it is today with television — or even in radio today. Radio was still new. It hadn't yet realized the extent to which it could exploit the public commercially. Commercial standards had not yet taken over. Advertising agencies were not yet as powerful as they later became. A man like myself could make some headway, and there was some opportunity. There were no such things as disc jockeys, no such things as telephone oracles who would ventilate their visions and prejudices.

BELL: Was the A.F.M. [American Federation of Musicians] ban on recorded music in effect then?

CORWIN: That came much later.

BELL: So there were disc jockeys, then.

CORWIN: Not in the modern sense.

BELL: Players of records.

CORWIN: Yes, but they did not come on the air with the kind of approach that is common today. In other words, they did not conceive of themselves as disc jockeys. They were programmers. Just as I, in my poetry program, would have conceived of myself as a kind of anthologist rather than as a personality with side comments and entertainment to jazz up the poems.

BELL: What percentage of the average hour was commercial time at that point?

CORWIN: It was relatively discreet.

BELL: Five to ten minutes?

CORWIN: In an hour? I would say in that range, yes — perhaps shading towards five. I don't think that greed and avarice and all of the negatives of broadcasting had yet become standard.

BELL: Was pirating a big problem at that time? Jamming? Was the FCC having trouble regulating the situation?

CORWIN: No, that came later. That was perhaps epitomized by the famous FCC *Blue Book*. I was, by the way, the direct beneficiary of that whole passage in radio history. The *Blue Book* gave me my start, really, in any important way, by scaring the networks into doing something conscionable. The *Blue Book* was based on a study of the abuses of commercial radio. When it came out, the networks were jolted. They were very much afraid that the government would take over and control broadcasting as they did in Britain.

BELL: Do you feel that this was a legitimate fear?

CORWIN: I don't think there was much chance of that happening. But that's hindsight. I don't fault the broadcasters for being apprehensive. I'm awfully glad they were. I, for one, was, and still am, a proponent of very strict regulation as to the amount of commercial time — and in relation to the ethics of broadcasting. I don't think we've ever passed beyond the need for that.

BELL: You did newspaper work for ten or twelve years?

CORWIN: Well, newspaper work for eight years and then PR work for the next two, two plus — for Twentieth Century-Fox Films, for the greater glory of Don Ameche, Sonja Henie, Shirley Temple, Bill Robinson, Tyrone Power.

BELL: Did you have any contact with Zanuck or the other producers, personally?

CORWIN: None, because I had nothing to do with production. Bear in mind that this was the home office of Twentieth Century-Fox, on East 56th Street in New York. I was a member of the publicity department under a man named Charles McCarthy and a lieutenant under him named Earl Wingate.

We would repair to the theater — there was a theater in this building and quite a good one — and two or three times a week, or as often as there was new product shipped in from the coast, we would sit down and see these films because we were going to be writing about them. I remember thinking how wonderful it was to be seeing all these movies and getting paid for it. Anyhow, that lasted until such time as CBS invited me to join their staff as a director.

BELL: You petitioned for that PR job, or were you approached for it?

CORWIN: The PR job was the direct result of the kindly and brotherly intercession of one of my two brothers, Emil. He was working for the publicity department at NBC at that time, and he knew about the opening. At that time, I was still a newspaper reporter, sometime editor, sometime columnist, sometime broadcaster for the *Springfield Republican*. I went down to New York, had an interview with Leonard Gaynor at Fox, and was engaged. I was quite happy there — a nice bunch of people and good writers, some of them later developed independent credits writing for *The New Yorker* and organs like that.

BELL: Was there disdain for the job?

CORWIN: There is a tendency for a man to justify his job. I think that even a man on a dump truck — witness Carlo

Tranghese — has pride in his work, has a rationale for it. Some-one has to keep the city clean, and he was doing that noble task.

I don't want to exaggerate. I don't want to imply that I considered PR work the same as hauling garbage, but at the same time it is not one of man's grander enterprises. The work at Fox was pleasant in many ways — one of them being that it at last got me up to $50 a week, a figure that had eluded me for the first twenty-six years of my life.

Each week I'd prepare a 15-minute sheaf of copy called "Broadcasting News," and it was for distribution to radio stations throughout the country. It was carefully scripted palaver that, in an offhand way, plugged Fox pictures and the people in them. It was intended to be read on the air at each station to which the broadcasting letter was addressed, read by the local gossiper, the movie columnist, or anybody who had access to a microphone.

For this work, my background in translating news copy right off the wires, into radioese, was of help to me. It was good for the "Broadcasting Newsletter" and also for Gregory Ratoff and The Ritz Brothers and Jane Withers and Jean Hersholt and Janet Gaynor and Simone Simone and Sidney Blackmer and Annabella. It was not written to be excessively simple, but certainly to be assimilable by the lowest talent. Not dumb, you understand.

I saved a whole sheaf of that stuff and read it over four or five years ago when I stumbled across it in an old carton. It held up pretty well. I don't have to be chagrined about that phase of work as I do about some others.

Another benefit of that job was feeding people and myself at the expense of Twentieth Century-Fox since one of my mis-sionary duties was to make friends with the editors of film-trade journals and various people in broadcasting who were in a position to do Fox a good turn every now and then. The boon of free meals was a new experience, a luxury that seemed to me at the time to be verging on decadence because I ate in posh restaurants that I would not have patronized on my own power. It was no longer chow at the hash joint or dinner at the diner. It was eating — eating underscored.

I think I got savvy pretty fast; and one of my jobs was to meet incoming stars, directors, and producers and see that they got transportation from Grand Central or from the dock when they arrived on a transoceanic liner. I would meet them, take them at Fox expense in taxis to their hotels. Somebody had to represent Twentieth Century-Fox, and on those occasions it was I.

This contact with celebrity was brief and perfunctory. They took no notice of me, except that once I met Loretta Young, and she said to her friend, "Ah, doesn't he remind you of Father Brown?" I don't know who Father Brown was, but certainly I did not cut an ecclesiastical figure. It was a nice interim. It served to get me to New York and to meet with people who were in show biz, and that was a little bit of a head start toward what I was soon to engage in as a director and writer for CBS.

BELL: Wasn't it around this time that you proposed a poetry program to WQXR?

CORWIN: Yes. I phoned the station one day, proposed an idea for a series to be called *Poetic License,* was invited to come to the studio and audition it, and did — on a lunch break. They liked what they heard and offered me 9:15 to 9:30 Tuesday nights. Since WQXR was not rich (this was years before the *New York Times* bought it) they said they couldn't pay me anything. Hell, I thought the price was right, and so launched the series while I continued working at Fox. It soon enlisted the interest of the best poets in the East, and some appeared as guests. It was innovative, I'll say that for it.

Chapter 2

BELL: How did you come to the attention of CBS?

CORWIN: It worked like this: My brother Emil, who had long ago constituted a committee of one to boost his kid brother, was then working in the press department at NBC, and he persuaded a colleague named Ted Church — T. Wells Church — to listen to my stuff on WQXR. One night, after I directed and produced what was the first radio adaptation of *Spoon River Anthology* — a fifteen-minute truncation, if you can believe it — I got a phone call from Ted, whom I had previously met through Emil. I was still at the station. Ted said, "Would you be interested in directing the *Columbia Workshop*?"

I thought he meant a workshop at Columbia University which was right around the corner from where I was living. I didn't get it right away. Then I realized he was talking about radio and CBS. Ted was a close friend of Bob Trout, and Bob's fiancée was the secretary of Bill Lewis. Do you follow the trail?

BELL: Yes.

CORWIN: Church asked Bob Trout's fiancée to mention me to Bill Lewis. So it was an inside track. It went from my brother Emil to Ted Church to Bob Trout's girl to Lewis.

It was through a series of serendipitous breaks that I came to the notice of the network. Bob Trout's and my tracks converged again in London when I went over there to do the *American in England* series. On hand to meet me at Charing Cross station was Bob — this was during a blackout, when it was very hard to get taxis. Trout and Kitty, now his wife, came to the train station and flagged down a taxi to get me to the Savoy. I saw a good deal of Bob during the months that I spent in London doing the *American in England* series.

BELL: Did CBS hire you for your writing?

CORWIN: CBS engaged me as a director. They knew nothing about my writing. The vice-president in charge of programming heard one of my programs, and I was engaged. I knew I was a writer, but they did not. I kept that knowledge to myself, pretty much. And for a period of four or five months, I directed what I was assigned to direct. That consisted of various programs, including a series called *Americans at Work* which dealt with great occupational areas in America — railroading, automobile manufacturing, agriculture, and so on.

BELL: Was this a documentary show, or was it written and then reenacted?

CORWIN: It was reenacted — yes. But it was not, however, docudrama. There was no story line.

BELL: A montage of impressions?

CORWIN: Pretty much, yes. I enjoyed it. I loved the medium; and by directing this and other programs, I became familiar with the console, the control board, and how to relate to engineers and sound men and the entire production staff. I also became acquainted with actors — learned who they were and what they could do. I became familiar with the resources.

BELL: Do you remember who wrote those shows?

CORWIN: Yes, some of them were written by Margaret Lerwerth and some by Charles R. Jackson who later was famed for *The Lost Weekend.* He wrote the novel that became the movie and won an Oscar. There were other writers, free-lancers mostly and not staff people, who contributed scripts.

Then at one point I was asked to be guest director of the *Columbia Workshop.* It was then called an experimental pro-gram. By today's lights it might not be considered terribly experimental, but it was certainly interested in new forms, and it broke new ground. It had a high standing, not only at CBS, but in the industry. There was a certain cachet about it. It proudly held itself above any proprietary interest. In other words, it was not the property of any one director or producer or writer. When you received an invitation to write or direct the *Workshop,* that was like being invited to an audience with the Queen.

BELL: Who did the inviting, specifically?

CORWIN: That was done by Bill Lewis, probably — with the input of Max Wylie, who was the head of continuity and scripts, and Douglas Coulter, who was assistant to Bill Lewis.

BELL: Was this a Sunday afternoon program?

CORWIN: I don't think it was a Sunday afternoon program. I think it was a weekday program. I may be wrong. Certainly the records will show which it was. We're talking about 1938, 1939. I joined the network late in '38.

BELL: What was the state of radio drama in the early 1930s?

CORWIN: There were no technical problems with actors and musicians. Again, in retrospect, much of what they did sounds limited today; but conceptually it took a while for radio drama to discover, to grow into the medium. For a time the microphone did not move in radio, just as the camera did not move in the early movies. Everything came before the microphone and was played as though you had an immovable camera. In this sense, early radio drama simply took stage plays and adapted them. A narrator read the business that was in the script. "Act One is set in a home in the Michigan peninsula. The Joneses have been away, and their maid is expecting them. The phone rings, and she answers it." Then she goes to the telephone, and you are on your way.

BELL: Did they feel limited to a single setting in a single program and not trust the audience to follow scenic changes without sight?

CORWIN: No, I don't think it was a matter of not trusting the audience's capacity to follow, but a matter of the naivete of the writer who wasn't aware of what he could do. He was not yet trained to use the listener as a collaborator and to play on his imagination.

BELL: Was it the comedy programs that began to show the dramatists what they could do?

CORWIN: No, it may have been the other way around — the dramatists showing the comedy programs what they could do.

BELL: What programs do you recall beginning to stretch things out?

CORWIN: The programs of Irving Reis and my own, principally. I think Bill Robson was part of that. I don't know where Oboler came in that succession. He may have preceded me. I don't know, but I was so busy writing my own things that I didn't have a chance to listen to what others were doing.

I think — though I'd much rather a third party made this judgment — that in the interest of fairness to myself and in going by what the historians of the medium have found, I may very well have been in the vanguard of that whole business of exploiting and enlarging the techniques. Indeed, there is either a master's or doctoral thesis in which someone mentions my influence on commercials. It refers to the cold opening which had not before been tried. I opened programs cold, ahead of announcements, ahead of music sometimes. This was attention-grabbing, not in any sensational way but in a way that would at least pique the interest of the listener.

There have been a number of studies — some of which the authors have sent me or which were published, eight or nine pieces — based upon what was considered my innovative work. I say this not in any vain way. I was lucky to have come along when I did, and I think that had it not have been me, it would have been any number of people.

There were quite striking and formidable programs done before I launched my series on CBS. *Fall of the City* came before I did. I think I was already at CBS when it was done, but *Fall of the City* was a major program and a benchmark in the history of radio drama. It wasn't as though you could go out and get a cassette or recording of those things. Radio was very slow to realize the archival value of its product.

BELL: What was the most important thing about *Fall of the City*?

CORWIN: Largely, the concept and the language and the use it made of its materials. The physical proportions of it were enormous. It was done in an armory, and there were three or four directors for that program, operating simultaneously. As one reads the text of *Fall of the City* today, it stands up as poetry; but there are certain locutions, certain mannerisms, that seem quite dated and a little stiff. MacLeish's next play, *Air Raid*, mostly avoided these mannerisms and was in my view more radiogenic, but this may be splitting hairs. In any case it enjoyed the benefit of Bill Robson's direction, and he was one of the best men around.

It was sometime later — I don't think it was more than a few weeks later — that I did *They Fly Through the Air*, which was only my second original script, the first having been *The Plot to Overthrow Christmas*. When I did *They Fly Through the Air*, Bill Robson, who after all had a proprietary interest in *Air Raid*, came into the studio after the broadcast and told me that he thought that it did a better job with a similar theme.

I was stunned by that appraisal; and in later years, when I reread *Fall of the City* in preparation for an article that the Museum of Broadcasting asked me to write, I was much taken by the beauty of MacLeish. I was a fan of his anyway.

I was not particularly influenced by him, but I admired his thrust, and I think *Fall of the City* holds up beautifully. But I also know what Robson meant — that mine was a more assimilable script.

BELL: Do you say assimilable in a positive sense?

CORWIN: Yes, metaphysics requires a special audience. It's not a dish for everybody. I am by nature and instinct an anti-obscurantist. I have very small patience with writers who need to be interpreted by a board of interpreters before you can understand what the hell they are talking about.

Many men whose work I greatly admire have innings where they are undecipherable. I'm much more tolerant of abstraction in other fields of art — painting and sculpture — they are not *lingua francas* to the extent that written and spoken language is, but a subtler form of communication.

I must say that notwithstanding the metaphysical properties of many great works, they can be beautiful and enduring. You have to discriminate between the book of *The Magic Flute* and the music of *The Magic Flute*. The music is universal, assimilable, and immortal. The book is trash.

Chapter 3

BELL: I recently read a script that you and Lucille Fletcher had written together called *My Client Curley*. Whose concept was that?

CORWIN: It was entirely her concept of the dancing caterpillar. However, she kept the action entirely in Hollywood. I was pressed by Douglas Coulter of CBS into adapting and producing Lucy's unpublished short story. At the time, I was not particularly keen to do it. I was very disturbed by what was going on in the world, and my tendency was to write the kind of radio better represented by *They Fly Through the Air*. Here, I thought, was a piece of cotton candy. But Coulter persuaded me that the world was entitled to relax every now and then. He didn't have to twist my arm very hard. I took it on and changed a great deal in it. All of the complications, the musicologist and the scientists, those were mine.

BELL: That seemed to me to be the case. But the other end — the Hollywood, PR side — was hardly something that you were unfamiliar with. You worked on *Columbia Workshop* from 1938 to 1941, correct?

CORWIN: I worked on *Columbia Workshop* sporadically before 1941.

BELL: Were those your only duties at the time?

CORWIN: Oh, no. I directed *County Seat*, my one contact with soap opera, a serial written by Milton Geiger. Orson Welles introduced the first episode because his friend, Ray Collins, was the star. It was about a small-town pharmacist, which I think Geiger had been. Then I did work occasionally for *School of the Air*, and I did my first adaptations of Carl Sandburg. The first radio adaptation of *The People, Yes* came on that program — a daytime program. Then I did a series of documentaries called *Americans at Work*.

I directed only. Indeed, I was directing one of those programs in a studio just above the one occupied by Orson Welles and the Mercury Theatre of the Air — the night they did the Mars show. I followed them on the air.

BELL: Were there disruptions?

CORWIN: No, we didn't know in our studio what had happened. What happened, of course, was that Orson Welles and crew had emptied all the living rooms of America, so that my broadcast, I'm sure, was heard by a very small audience.

BELL: When was his famous press conference?

CORWIN: The next day.

BELL: How closely on the heels of *Words Without Music* did *26 by Corwin* follow?

CORWIN: There were many intervening projects. One of them was *Pursuit of Happiness*. That was 1939. Burgess

Meredith was the MC. It was on that program that we did *Ballad for Americans,* a sort of seminal program.

BELL: We have yet to mention a series called *Living History* which is reportedly the first that you directed at CBS.

CORWIN: I directed that but never wrote it.

BELL: That series and *Americans at Work* were both produced by Gilbert Seldes.

CORWIN: He was a nice man — a bit on the fussy side. Meticulous, pleasant, knowledgeable. I believe he was associated with the first salient of CBS into television. He left the radio scene and went over to the Grand Central studios of CBS, I think. We did not have much contact after that. I am mentioned in his book, *The Great Audience,* but I can't recall in what context. It's a passing reference.

BELL: I remember the book as a comparative book on different media.

CORWIN: Yes, one of the first sociological studies of radio and television.

BELL: Didn't he assign radio the place of some mysterious, oracular function which he thought inherently fascist?

CORWIN: That the medium was inherently fascist?

BELL: He seemed to think it was a perfect tool of fascist states for mental subjection because the speaker is hidden, like the man behind the curtain in *The Wizard of Oz,* and because the conveyance is the word, a flexible and hypnotic thing.

CORWIN: I must say that if that was his thesis, then I would quarrel with it at this late stage. I give you the example of a society, in one of the Polynesian or Melanesian islands, where its parliament had the custom of turning its back on the person addressing them, so they would not be influenced by his face or gestures. I thought that was a highly sophisticated attitude. I would disagree with Seldes on that very sharply. One pays much more attention to what is being said if one doesn't see the face. There are very great dangers of pretty-boys winning elections on the strength of their charismatic, B-picture images.

BELL: Was there some kind of set process for earning one's stripes at CBS in the early '40s?

CORWIN: I was the beneficiary of the extraordinary bounty and largesse of William B. Lewis, vice-president in charge of programming. He had hired me, and I simply went to Bill one day and said that I had an idea for a program. He made available the funds, a very modest budget — like $200 or $300 — to make a little pilot recording.

I did it, and he liked it. He scheduled it for Sunday afternoons, right after the New York Philharmonic concerts. It was he who proposed the title and who proposed the proprietary billing — *Norman Corwin's Words Without Music*. I wasn't crazy about that title, but you don't argue with the boss, especially when he's giving you a wonderful opportunity.

Now, as far as procedure is concerned — how I won my chevrons — it was simply the success of these programs. That's the only way I can put it. The first script I wrote was

The Plot to Overthrow Christmas, and that got a lot of attention. Four or five weeks later, I did *They Fly Through the Air* which won the then highest award for radio drama for the year, the Ohio State Award, in the days before the Peabody or anything else. Suddenly you find you are written up in the *World-Telegram* and *Time,* and that creates a certain status. Automatically — without conferences and negotiations and memoranda — you now enjoy recognition; and that recognition very quickly transfers from the audience and the press to the 18th floor at CBS and the 22nd as well.

BELL: Mr. Lewis was a very well-regarded man in general by the radio scene. What did he do after he left CBS?

CORWIN: When we got into the war, he left CBS — at first on loan to the government, to the Office of Facts and Figures where he was associated with Archibald MacLeish. Then he went from there to commercial radio, and was, I think, chief of Kenyon and Eckhart for quite a number of years. Then, I believe, he had some connection with the American Red Cross. Of course I *know* that Frank Stanton did because he was president of the Red Cross for a long time.

BELL: How many programs was *Words Without Music?*

CORWIN: Twenty-six. But most of those were adaptations. The whole premise of the program, initially, was not as a vehicle for my own work. It was conceived as something in which I would bring to the public the neglected literature of poetry, and I took some of the classics and adapted them.

BELL: Which plays?

CORWIN: I have a volume of bound scripts right here, and I'm just going to run over that. I'm going to give you the names of the poets, and if you want, I'll specify the particular poem. There was Longfellow, Whitman, Robert Frost, W. S. Gilbert, Amy Lowell. I did an amusing program called *Broadway Document* that was put together by Edward Mayehoff. Mayehoff was a very original comedian, superb in delivery, and in the writing of his own material. I'll be damned if I know what happened to Ed Mayehoff. It's one of the great mysteries.

BELL: A Broadway comedian?

CORWIN: Not in the sense of being on the stem, but he *was* New York City. His work was rich in all of the best elements of caricature and satire without getting into the Mort Sahl or Lenny Bruce vein. It wasn't savage; it wasn't mordant; but he had a kind of wonderfully perceptive, warm, sympathetic eye and ear for eccentrics and for the people you would meet along Broadway.

BELL: He worked the New York vein exclusively?

CORWIN: Yes, as far as I know. And I also did a piece called *Murder in Studio One,* and he was on that program and played a character named Elwin Repell. It was ninety percent Mayehoff. Anybody interested in seeing what his style was like, I refer to that script.

BELL: Where did *Murder in Studio One* come from?

CORWIN: Well, I met Ruth Gordon through the Laughtons. She, of course, was a wonderful comic, and I wrote a show for her. I just thought it would be fun to have a woman sleuth, whom I called Cameo Klopf.

BELL: Who were some of the other poets in *Words Without Music*?

CORWIN: Vachel Lindsay, William Rose Benet, Carl Sandburg, Robert Francis, Edward Lear, and Oliver Wendell Holmes. I would sneak in one or two of my own, not in my name, but with a pseudonym. I felt I had no right to thrust myself, by name, among people of the heft and quality of Thackeray and Bret Harte.

BELL: What was the response to your scripts?

CORWIN: On the slight pieces there was no response. But my first original was *The Plot to Overthrow Christmas*, and that got a lot of response. Indeed, that was how I met Edward R. Murrow. The morning after that was broadcast — Christmas fell on a Sunday that year, and Monday I was in my office — there was a knock on my door, and it was Murrow, whom I had never met. He was then European chief, based in London but home for the holidays. He told me that he and his wife had listened to the play the night before, and hadn't had as much fun listening to verse since last hearing W. S. Gilbert.

BELL: Is that play done often?

CORWIN: Yes, it's been done many times over the years. Now here is one of the *Words Without Music* scripts. Let's see — Alfred Noyes is represented. And James Weldon Johnson.

BELL: Who's he?

CORWIN: A black poet who wrote verse, though it was "negro" then. Also represented is Thomas Hood, Shakespeare, Matthew Arnold, Jonathan Swift.

BELL: Was the format of those plays something like a breaking apart of the verse — or a dramatizing of it?

CORWIN: I dramatized them, but in doing so I broke them up, being as careful as I could to do no disservice or damage to the original. If I interpolated, I tried to do it within the style of the poet. One can imitate without doing great damage because that is like the copyist who goes into a museum and does an almost photographic copy of a great painting. There's no great trick to that. One could botch it, of course, by being inept. But I was careful.

This is confirmed by the response that I got from schools and colleges where teachers of English and literature complimented me for being able to interest their students in this kind of writing. When they found this stuff being done with sound and by good actors, they were attracted to it. Many of these teachers would assign their classes to listen to the program. If I had done violence to the source material, you can be sure I would have heard protests. Not only that, but the living poets who were on this series were very happy to have their work done. Also, they got a modest fee for the use of the stuff.

Indeed, when I did a *Spoon River Anthology* half hour, Edgar Lee Masters was in the city at the time. I invited him to come to the studio, and he did. I seated him in the sub-control room. I didn't want him to be in the control room because he would be distracted by all of the technical appa-ratus and the voices and conversation that attended the broadcast. During the course of the broadcast, I noticed that my actors were looking toward the sub-control room and then dropping their eyes or looking away. I wondered what the hell that meant, but I didn't have time to speculate very long on that because we were going from line to line.

When the program was over, I opened the door to the sub-control room; and there was Edgar Lee Masters dissolved in tears, very much shaken. My actors had been embarrassed to look at him. They stole glances.

When he recovered, he said to me that the people upon whom he based *Spoon River Anthology* were real people, people he knew. Uncannily, he said, the actors sounded like them as they spoke their words. He had never seen or heard these works enacted before. I may have been the first to make any such dramatization of *Spoon River Anthology*. There have been many productions since, but I was the first, I think. That was a new experience for Masters, and he was much moved by it. After he recovered, he met with the cast and autographed scripts for them. It was a beautiful, beautiful occasion.

BELL: You have worked with Mr. Erik Barnouw.

CORWIN: Yes, I have.

BELL: Was he involved in radio writing for very long?

CORWIN: He was, off and on, but he's had a varied and distinguished career since then, doing all kinds of things. He was a professor at Columbia. He was custodian of the Library of Congress's media department. In fact, he wrote the foreword to R. LeRoy Bannerman's biography of me. He's also represented in the book *Thirteen for Corwin*.

Anyway, Barnouw wrote for *Pursuit of Happiness*, and I directed it and contributed a few things of my own. It was a sustaining program — Bill Lewis's concept I think — that stated its purpose in this way, as spoken originally by Burgess Meredith in the opening show:

"This is a show about the United States of America — of American things and American places and American people. We'll take a look at the goings-on among the citizens of this republic as they bear on the exercise of that third inalienable right, the right to chase rainbows."

We took advantage of stars who were going through New York or coming back from Europe or in town for this or that occasion. Our top fee was $500. We had agents always on the lookout for who was coming into town and who would be available, and we booked them. It was up to me and Barnouw and others in the backfield to match material.

It was a resourceful program with a lot of music — illustrated handsomely by *Ballad for Americans* — and furbished with stars like Fredric March and Danny Kaye. I believe this was Kaye's first appearance on radio. He got $50 for his performance.

BELL: He was a nightclub comedian then?

CORWIN: Yes, at that time. Also, there was Imogene Coca, Carl Carmer, an orchestra conducted by Mark Warnow, and sometimes a chorus.

I prepared some elements of Stephen Vincent Benét's *John Brown's Body* for Charles Laughton and directed him in that.

Abbott and Costello were in the series. Then there was William Saroyan, Jimmy Durante, and Walter Huston. So you see, it had quite a range.

BELL: This was at the time of Saroyan's greatest popularity.

CORWIN: Yes, right.

BELL: Did he write for you or read his own material?

CORWIN: He wrote a script for which he was paid $200.

BELL: How were the ratings?

CORWIN: The ratings I don't remember. It was at 4:30 to 5:00 on Sundays. Not prime time.

BELL: Wasn't Sunday, afternoon particularly, considered the bad day in the week back then?

CORWIN: I don't know whether it was a ghetto or not. I suppose that, even then, it was a kind of intellectuals' ghetto. This is how I met my first stars, though. Some became lifelong friends, like Freddie March and the Laughtons.

BELL: How did you work on characterization on the radio stage?

CORWIN: I was never conscious of any method. I proceeded by instinct, not the product of any method or school. I had never studied that medium but had been a novice when I did my first program on WBZA. I simply flew by the seat of my pants.

BELL: Were you often taking direction from those you were working with — the more experienced actors or technicians?

CORWIN: No. But I wasn't a martinet. My productions, I'm glad to say, were happy. They were marked by geniality. I think I had pretty good luck in casting, and that simplified matters. My view of the actor was never that of an instrument that I was playing but that of an instrumentalist who was an artist in his own right. If he had a suggestion to make, and I liked it, I was very happy to get it and use it. But that did not often occur.

When I cast something I have written, I know what I want, and the right actor is half the battle or more. After that choice, it is usually just a matter of some minor adjustment in approach. Rarely was the problem of interpretation spread out over days of rehearsal. We didn't have days; we had hours. Everything was compressed in time — compared to film or theatre.

BELL: What was the casting apparatus at CBS?

CORWIN: It was never through a casting office. When I became a director, word quickly got around to the then relatively small acting community; and I received calls and letters asking for appointments to be auditioned. I would meet these people, talk with them. On this subject, have you read the piece that I wrote just recently for AFTRA's 50th anniversary?

BELL: No, I didn't.

CORWIN: Then let me read it to you. It answers your question. The article is titled: "Reflections on Civility and the Art of Bad-mouthing."

"One day in my twenty-eighth year, by steps too many and luck too freakish to recount here, I found myself for the first time in a position to employ people. Actors. I had just become a radio director at CBS. It was before the dawn of AFRA [American Federation of Radio Artists], and even then there were more actors looking for work than there were jobs. And because broadcast drama was then relatively new, and programs relatively few, the emergence of a new director anywhere along the route was of interest to the profession. Actors began calling and writing for appointments and for a chance to audition.

"Having always been a seeker and not a giver of jobs, I identified with the applicants. Some, especially the hungriest, were nervous — not because I was forbidding, but because I had the power to hire. I had been a publicity flack a few weeks earlier, and before that, a newspaperman, and in both capacities I was no more capable of inspiring apprehension than a frozen haddock. But now I could assign paying roles, and that made me someone to reckon with. Actors asked each other about me as they did about every new director. Was I easy to meet? Did one have to wait long for an appointment? Did I furnish audition material, or must one bring one's own?

"Out of empathy I would not stay behind the desk in my office but came around and sat in front of it to equalize spatially the terms of meeting — not as a point of strategy, but out of interest. I talked of unrelated matters before getting down to the purpose of the interview. Usually, when the visitor saw that I took interest in him as a person, and not just as a hireable type, the onus of having to sell himself, always a strain, tended to vanish; and I could get a truer impression of qualities that might be helpful in a studio.

"I never had reason to change my outlook on actors. They are not as a class the easiest company, especially if they enjoy international celebrity or have been fanned and petted and inflated by stardom. But the young, talented actor — unfossilized by doctrine or method, eager to learn and put his learning to work — is a joy to the playwright and director. So is the star who keeps his head when all about him are wrangling over contracts, publicity, co-casting, billing, agents, managers, schedules, and the rest of the distractions in Pandora's makeup box. It may be quaintness, but I have always regarded actors and actresses as collaborators, not puppets. All but a few justify that outlook; and the exceptions tend to be those whose insecurity may be so deep, or whose training so doctrinaire, that they are difficult for most, if not all, directors.

"To me the cardinal no-no of directing is hauteur. I have only contempt for producers and directors, in whatever medium, who treat job-seeking actors, singers, and dancers as if they were robots dismissable by the flip of a switch. To interrupt an audition literally in mid-sentence with a cold, "Thank you, that's all!" is unforgivable. It takes very little time to be considerate, to honor common courtesy and, at no cost to management, protect the dignity of the artist. Even the untalented have a right to be treated civilly and not as some kind of cattle mistakenly let in from a pen. Perhaps even more unforgivable than rudeness in auditions is abusiveness in rehearsals.

"I once watched a major film director, frustrated because he could not get what he wanted from a pair of stars of the first magnitude, take it out on a bit player — a violent tongue-lashing over a picky, arbitrary matter — in front of the whole company. It can be argued that genius has certain prerogatives, that artistic tyranny can be justified by results; but that is a cop-out. An acting, musical, or dance company is not a boot camp for military recruits, and it has yet to be demonstrated that a production of any kind will turn out better if the director is a son-of-a-bitch.

"Of course, artists are not without sin either; but unless they own the studio, their sins do not carry the same weight as those exercised by authority. One of the singular features of radio drama, incidentally, was that its casts would assemble, read, rehearse, and go on the air — all within a few hours, so that there was no time for neurotic frills, intramural intrigues, backstage bickering, or general moodiness.

"I have experienced only two or three destructive artists in all my years in the media, and they only in the theatre — the kind who, having time to incubate some sort of conspiracy, work against the interests of the play or against other actors to gain some dubious personal advantage. But most of the species is wonderfully awake and aware, talented, dedicated, hard-working, inquiring, considerate — as treasurable to the playwright and director as a master performer to a composer and conductor.

"Still, over the long run I wish most actors and actresses had better opinions of themselves. I bridle whenever they are assisted in self-deprecation by such troglodytes as the late Westbrook Pegler who scorned singers and actors because 'a singer emits certain sounds from the neck, that's all . . . An actor utters recitations written for him; he bawls, whimpers or whispers, and stands here and there according to minute directions after long and patient instruction.'

"It is one thing for a non-actor like Pegler to say such things, or for Samuel Johnson, who had serious reservations even about Shakespeare, to denigrate players as 'no better than creatures set upon tables and stools to make faces and produce laughter, like dancing dogs,' or for the wry Oliver Herford to say, with better humor, 'Actresses will happen in the best of families.' But it is another thing for actors to dump on themselves, as when Richard Burton told an interviewer, 'You may be as vicious as you please. You will only do me justice.' Or when Bing Crosby summed himself up by saying, 'I think I've stretched a talent which is so thin it's opaque' — he meant transparent — 'over an unenviable term of years.'

"Tallulah Bankhead advised a young woman, 'If you want to help the American theatre, darling, don't be an actress, be an audience.' Cedric Hardwicke speculated that 'God felt sorry for actors so He created Hollywood to give them a place in the sun and a swimming pool. The price they had to pay was to surrender their talent.' I'm afraid Orson Welles summed it up when he confessed, 'Every actor in his heart believes everything bad that's said about him.' That may be, but it is no reason for the artist to add to his burden by saying bad things about himself. There is enough rudeness in hiring halls and casting calls without voluntary contributions from members of the organization whose anniversary we honor and in whose publication this appears. It will never hurt you to believe everything *good* that's said about you, too."

BELL: That's good. What was the size of your technical staff on the typical broadcast of the time?

CORWIN: A studio engineer, of course, and a production assistant, who mainly kept the stopwatch, and as many sound men as were required, which averaged, depending on the demands of the script, two.

BELL: Did you work with more than three mikes frequently?

CORWIN: Oh yes, I've worked with as many as eight mikes. That would include a remote studio as well, in which the orchestra had to perform on occasion. That wasn't often, but there were occasions when I picked up from remotes. In *On a Note of Triumph*, the broadcast originated from Hollywood, but Bill Shirer was in San Francisco, and we brought him in, live, on cue.

BELL: Was there a preference of the actors, generally, to work in as compact a setting as possible — near the musicians and the sound men?

CORWIN: No, they were so expert at what they were doing that it didn't make any difference. In some cases when they were not essentially radio actors but stars who came in from some other medium, it helped them to have the music in the same studio with them. In the case of Charles Laughton, he was irked. He felt that the music overwhelmed him at one point. I disabused him of that attitude, and there was no problem.

BELL: Did you try not to work with movie stars?

CORWIN: I had no prejudice against movie stars. While I didn't go out after them, unless I was requested to do so or the occasion demanded, I always regarded it as helpful in that it would increase the size of the audience.

BELL: You used as many Broadway people as movie people.

CORWIN: If you're talking about week-to-week, yes. But for the special shows, they were full of stars. I refer you to the *Bill of Rights Show* and *Document A/777*.

BELL: You wrote in the introduction to the printed version, that this show, the *Bill of Rights Show* — or *We Hold These Truths* — was a very difficult one to write and conceive.

CORWIN: It was difficult to write because the canvas was so huge and there were also the superimposed requirements of an anniversary, the 150th anniversary of the ratification of that Bill of Rights. This meant that you had to have more than a nodding acquaintance with the occasion. Since that time we've had the national bicentennial, and there has been the anniversary of the Constitution, so the areas that have been so richly mined since that day had not been much explored at the time I did that program. I could not get from the libraries the kind of material I wanted. I was in Washington when I began working on it and got permission to stay in the Library of Congress after closing hours. The work was under such pressure that I had to do that. I went through the stacks and tried to find transcripts of those early hearings and committees and all the plumbing that went into the arrival at the Bill of Rights.

BELL: Does much exist?

CORWIN: It was pretty hard to find. It existed, but it was one hell of a headache trying to put it together. Nobody had, to my knowledge, done it. This isn't to say that I broke any ground, but that I had trouble pulling it together in the limited time. Scholars who have a year or two to work on a book are not harried and don't have a date facing them. That was the one fixed thing, the one specific tangible, from the day I agreed to do the program. That was it. I knew the day — December 15, 1941. Any start on that project later than six months in advance was already late, and I started it quite late. Not through any delinquency of my own, but that's when I was apprised of the project. Bill Lewis was in Washington by this time, and he was the man who approached me to do it.

It was a chaotic time. Pearl Harbor was bombed only eight days before this broadcast. In fact, I was on a train travelling from New York to Hollywood, still working on the script when the attack on Pearl Harbor took place. I was on the Santa Fe *Chief*, and when it reached Kansas City — I had maybe forty-five minutes there before the train took off again — I tried to get through to Washington to find out whether the state of war was going to change everything. The President was scheduled to be on the program, and I had shaped it so that it would accommodate him at the end. Also, all of the regularly scheduled programs of December 7th were preempted, completely taken over with war news until a certain hour in the evening. Anyway, I couldn't get through to Washington. All the lines were busy, so I sent a telegram. When I got to Albuquerque, there was a reply. They had asked the President, and he had said that it was more important than ever that this program be done. That heartened me. The script would have been a lot of wasted effort otherwise.

BELL: Do you have a transcript of the program with the President's speech following?

CORWIN: I don't have it, nor is it appended to any published version of my script — and there are several. But the speech exists in the presidential papers. It was a nondescript speech, not organically connected with the program. Unfortunately, FDR never even heard the program. I was told that he was surprised the next day to learn what kind of fireworks had preceded him because the program made a very great impact. If it were any good at all, it could hardly fail to make some sort of impression since every network station in the country carried it. It was an all-network show, the first of its kind.

BELL: You used some contrapuntal dialogue in that show — overlapping.

CORWIN: Not a lot. But I used it where I thought it was needed.

BELL: Was that new for you?

CORWIN: Yes, I think I was among the first to make use of that.

Chapter 4

BELL: Tell me about *The Lonesome Train*.

CORWIN: *The Lonesome Train* was brought to me by Earl Robinson, its composer, not long after I had inaugurated the first of the *Columbia Presents Corwin* series. Robinson had previously scored a big hit in a program that I directed on the *Pursuit of Happiness* series called *Ballad for Americans*. As with *Ballad for Americans*, which I helped by making suggestions as to its shape and its title, I proposed changes in the score and the treatment of *The Lonesome Train*. I changed its title as well. Originally he called it *Lincoln Cantata*.

I said to Robinson, "You're not Johann Sebastian Bach. We live in an era when the cantata is not a viable form, and this is a folk piece. It's warm and about a folk hero and a genuine national treasure. You have already built into the lyrics the most important line — 'The lonesome train.' Why don't you use that for a title?" He did.

I also suggested a change in the way it opened, which he implemented, having to do with the use of a banjo in the expert hands of Pete Seeger.

It was a good production from start to finish. I was in top form. The orchestra was in top form, as was Mark Warnow who conducted. Lyn Murray, who arranged and directed the choral work, was in top form. It went without a hitch in a playhouse on Broadway before an audience.

47

BELL: What was the concept of the piece?

CORWIN: After Lincoln was assassinated, there was a funeral train that started in Washington, went up the eastern seaboard, then west to Springfield, Illinois. There was a tremendous outpouring of grief. The concept was the work of Millard Lampell, a masterpiece of a libretto, the thrust of which was that Lincoln was not on that train. Instead, in various episodes, he was at the bedside of a wounded soldier, in a negro church in Alabama, at a folk dance, or he was with some buddies and cronies telling jokes and spinning yarns.

It's a mix of history and legend and atmosphere. The use of the train motif was powerful. Great credit in the history of that piece should go to a man named Ralph Wilkinson who arranged it. At that time I don't believe Robinson was doing his own orchestrations.

I remember getting a call from Deems Taylor after that broadcast, agog at some of its production values. One such effect was not a simple cross-fade. It was a kind of double exposure, but clear on both ends.

That was number two or three in *Columbia Presents Corwin*. I only wish that I'd been able to open the series with it because the show that I did open it with was, on a scale of one to one hundred, maybe a thirty-four. *The Lonesome Train* was a hundred. It has enjoyed revivals every now and then, and I think that it will keep having them for a long time. I don't mean repeating the original broadcast. I don't think that's ever been done. It's been recorded subsequently by others. I believe even Bing Crosby did a version.

It's a famous piece and deservedly so, though it has certain shortcomings as did *Ballad for Americans*. In the light of the intervening years, the endings of both pieces are perhaps over-sentimentalized. But I think that even the

most cynical American would have to be extremely un-
charitable not to feel a certain patriotic rapport with the
elements of both plays.

When Franklin Delano Roosevelt died and was carried by
train from Georgia to Hyde Park, Eleanor Roosevelt wrote
later that the melody and words of *The Lonesome Train* kept
going through her mind as she rode on that train.

BELL: There were a lot of good programs on radio, not
only yours, that had to do with travelling, trains, the going
from one place to another.

CORWIN: Trains intrigued not only Thomas Wolfe, but
millions of Americans. It's a pity that later generations grew
up not knowing the sound of the steam engine. What they
hear now, if they hear anything, is a diesel horn. The old
whistle of the panting locomotive, the chug-chug and the
marvelous thunder of those old engines, the sound of those
trains flying across the rails is something that aroused all
kinds of romantic associations.

I was once sharing a taxicab with Aaron Copland, and we
were talking about music, and I mentioned trains.

I said, "A genius like you might have a lot of fun with a
timetable."

We barely have the expression anymore, timetable; but in
those days — that now seem so long ago, the '40s and '50s
— when you went across the country, there was a timetable.
They had all the stations and wonderful symbols: the suits
of the diamond and the heart and the club and the spade,
crosses and double crosses, stars and asterisks and daggers,
those marvelous typographical squiggles. It told you how
long a train stopped at a station and from where and
whether this was on Wednesdays or Fridays or all week
long. In them they used to speak of the time of departure of

a train as a sailing — sailing time, sailing date. I just loved that.

Copland looked at me as though I were absolutely raving mad. He said nothing. So much for my seminal effect on modern American music.

BELL: What was it like to have had such great success in such a powerful mass medium at such a young age?

CORWIN: I considered myself lucky, but never to the extent that I stopped to savor it or relish it.

BELL: Is that fatal?

CORWIN: No, but I think it's necessary to keep one's head and not to let evidences of fame, or having a high profile in the press, get to you. CBS had a very powerful and adroit publicity arm. I could have made a career of appearing as a guest on programs and participating in seminars and lecturing and all that sort of thing, but I never got swept into it. I was concerned with keeping up a standard of work; and that left no time for preening, had I wanted to, which I did not.

BELL: Your period of greatest critical and public acclaim climaxed with *On a Note of Triumph.*

CORWIN: CBS came to me in 1945 and said, "Would you prepare a broadcast to go on the night of victory in Europe?" That's all they asked. There were no specifications. It was up to me, and where the hell do you begin with a subject like that? I had written extensively about the war. The one thing I knew was that the war would not be over that night, that we would still be at war with Japan. In other words, this was victory only in Europe.

What would be the mood of the country? That was not easy to answer, and that program was not easy to write, even if the writing had not been of a certain special kind.

BELL: Still, wasn't the occasion perceived as celebrational. and wasn't that partly responsible for the impact of the program?

CORWIN: Yes. The program came along at a time of great emotion and was given a great deal of promotion by CBS. It was well done. It gave the thinking element of the country something that it could grab onto. It said, "Yeah, we've won. But who did we beat, and what does it mean?"

So people, I think, were grateful for that. That might explain the impact. To this day people stop me. I'll give you an instance. I was flying to London on a film project. We were halfway across the Atlantic in the middle of the night and people were trying to sleep. Since I was on film business, I was flying first-class. In those days, at least on that airline, the name of the passenger was on the back of his seat, like the name on an Academy-of-Honor chair or something. There was the name "Corwin." The captain of the ship came out of the cockpit to go to the john, and he walked back up the cabin and saw that everyone was asleep except me. He looked down and saw my name, and he stopped and said, "Are you by any chance related to Norman Corwin?" I said, "I am he."

His next words were a quote from *On a Note of Triumph*. He told me the circumstances under which he'd heard it. He had bought the book, and this was a good twenty years after the broadcast. Also, every time I met Keenan Wynn on the street or in a room, he would recite lines from *On a Note of Triumph.*

I could give you fifty examples of that kind of thing, which of course are very warming and rewarding and make you feel good. But it does underscore what you were saying about the conspicuousness of that work among the others. It happened to be a matter of timing, a product of a national mood that I had nothing to do with setting up, that I simply took advantage of, not in any exploitative way. It was my coming in at the right time with the right words. It benefitted from all my experience. It was the culmination of my production techniques which came together pretty happily considering that, unlike a movie, which is done over a period of weeks, the broadcast was done in a day.

I had matured into that, although I must say that *Untitled* still had good material in it, and an earlier program called *The Long Name None Could Spell* had a lot of good pages in it.

BELL: In your notes to *On a Note of Triumph* — you said that by the time you wrote the piece, you felt drained of the subject, that you had already said all that you had to say.

CORWIN: I felt that I had. Of course, there was much more to say.

BELL: Do you like to read that particular play again?

CORWIN: It's one of the few things of mine to which I can listen or which I can read without regretting a line or a scene to the point that I have to stop reading or shut off the playback. Too many of my things I cannot tolerate, cannot listen to. Some of them are, in the judgment of others, pretty good, but not in mine. They embarrass me, so I do not listen to them. I have destroyed scripts. Some of them, alas, were published, and there is no recalling those because they are in libraries. But I do get requests to perform some of my work, and I deny them. I will not sell them for production if I don't like them. I forgive myself because I was much younger and that was the way I wrote at the time. But one moves on. I prefer not to be represented, to the extent that I can control this, by inferior work.

BELL: Do you resent *On a Note of Triumph* itself, its place in your reputation?

CORWIN: No, no. I am content with it. There are only a few words and lines that I feel are weak. But I'm like a parent who has many children. I was and am particularly fond of a couple of my lighter plays. The very first script I wrote for CBS was a rhymed fantasy called *The Plot to Overthrow Christmas*, and then there was one that I did in 1945 — the same year that I did *On a Note of Triumph* — with Groucho Marx and Robert Benchley and Vincent Price and Keenan Wynn which was called *The Undecided Molecule*.

BELL: Do you own your transcriptions from those series?

CORWIN: I own my transcriptions, but I've never done anything about them.

BELL: *Untitled* was written eight or nine months before *On a Note of Triumph* and wrings about as much out of the personal situation of warfare as is possible for the form. The criticism that I most often hear of *On a Note of Triumph* is of its strident quality and mythic aspect.

CORWIN: *On a Note of Triumph* was celebratory. It had to be. You could not commit yourself to a program on victory in Europe without sounding a note of triumph. And I did sound that. I would have been remiss not to. But, at the same time, it was cautionary. Whereas, *Untitled* was a demanding and challenging program. It said, "What are you going to do about it — you who have survived this?"

Untitled dealt with one man, and *On a Note of Triumph* really is all men. It was a national victory.

BELL: Was Fredric March your initial choice to play Hank Peters?

CORWIN: Yes.

BELL: Did you get a lot of mail for *Untitled*?

CORWIN: I got a lot of reaction, but the mail was modest. The press paid a good deal of attention to it.

Vogue magazine carried some excerpts from it. And either *P.M.* or *The Compass* in New York printed the whole script, and the *Detroit Free Press*, or one of those midwestern papers, carried the whole script. Also, *Coronet* magazine carried the whole script. So it got a lot of attention. I'm happy to hear you say what you do say about *Untitled* because your feeling about my work corresponds with my own. Discriminating editors and journalists were aware that it had a kind of quality.

BELL: Tell me about the One World Award.

CORWIN: That was instituted by friends of Wendell Willkie after he died. Did I not give you the reprint of my speech to the sponsors of the flight after I returned?

BELL: No, you didn't.

CORWIN: Well, I'll give that to you now, and it will answer that particular question.

BELL: Could you tell me about the award itself?

CORWIN: Wendell Willkie, after he was defeated for the Presidency by FDR, was appointed by Roosevelt to be a kind of personal ambassador at large, to go around to the members of the United Nations — we were still at war, you understand — and to meet and counsel with them. He made that trip, and when he came back he wrote a book called *One World*, which sold a couple of million copies. To this day it is an important book.

Then Willkie died, untimely, in his forties.

The friends of Willkie were largely liberal Republicans. Willkie had made a remarkable transference from a spokesman for corporate America to a liberal position that was to the left of anyone who ever was born or died a Republican. He was mourned by a great many people, and friends of Willkie formed an organization called The Willkie Memorial of Freedom House. I don't know if Freedom House is still in existence, but it was important at that time. Then, the *New York Herald-Tribune*, which was a moderate Republican paper, also wanted to perpetuate the memory of Willkie, so between them they decided that they would give an award to that person in the media who, in their view, had contributed most to the concept of *One World* in a given year. I believe their first year's award went to Kent Cooper, the head of the Associated Press. Cooper did nothing with it — never went on the trip.

The second year's award went to me, and I was approached by the committee and asked if I would accept the award which consisted of a trip around the world. I said that, first of all, I was under contract to Mr. Paley and I couldn't take the trip unless I was given leave by CBS. Second, I didn't want to go around as a tourist or even a passive observer. I wanted to make it a working trip — to go abroad and interview people and return to do a series of programs based upon that.

They said, would you go to Mr. Paley and ask him to give you the release?

And I went to Paley and told him what this was about, and he said, "We're very proud that you've been given this award, and not only will we do what you've requested, but we'll pay for a sound man to accompany you, and we'll give you the equipment, and we'll deliver the good offices of our correspondents around the world." And CBS did just that.

BELL: Do you have any regrets about this project now?

CORWIN: I wish I had known as much then as I do now, but that can't be remedied. Yet, I have to say for myself, there are some awfully good things in it, not so much of my own doing as what I elicited from Pandit Nehru and J. B. Priestley and people like that around the world.

BELL: Given the concept, you had to believe the best.

CORWIN: Not necessarily believe the best but *seek* the best. The announced aim of the series was lived up to — "To seek evidences of *rapprochement*." The opposite was all too much in evidence.

BELL: Your hindsight might be too harsh, then.

CORWIN: I tend to be harsh, I think, in judgments of my own work. That trait can be a strength or a weakness. Strength in that it prevented me ever from getting a troublesome ego. I've worked, I think, soberly and industriously. On the other hand, if you don't have sufficient respect for your own work, it can tease away your confidence.

BELL: In being a successful popular artist in America, isn't it a blessing not to have to expend energy on ego-feeding?

CORWIN: To me, ego-stroking rewards and the compliments and praises and honors were like a Chinese dinner — enjoyed and digested and passed. Life is not a continual feast, and I guess I always returned to the workbench. I was at that bench so much that there wasn't time to savor or reflect or particularly *use* those ego-massaging things. I think my reservations about what I did on the *One World* trip are consistent with my reservations about what I did right along, with everything. I felt, with very few exceptions, that it could have been done better. That judgment is delivered completely from hindsight and from the standpoint of a man who is older and has learned more, or hopes he has learned more, about writing and about life.

I think I did not make the very best use I could have made of my opportunities, but that may be a harsh judgment, and I cannot rely on my subjective balance there. When I look at the record and look at the scripts and listen to the tapes of these *One World* programs, I really cannot fault myself too much. I think I did a pretty good job, once the net effect and substance trickles through the filter, because I did get good statements out of men like Clement Attlee and Nehru. Some other good statements I got from people were off the record, so I couldn't print them.

So, I guess I should stop being quite as harsh in my recollection of that series as I have, from time to time, been. I just get damned irked by reading or listening to anything of mine where there is a flaw or a series of flaws. I just wish they weren't there. I like to think that better men than I, artists of very high talent, felt the same way about their work; but that is cold comfort when I listen to or read something of mine that could have been better.

BELL: There were obviously some technical problems along the way.

CORWIN: I don't count those against myself.

BELL: Then, are you faulting yourself for a matter of flaws in your interpolation, in your posture, in the interpretation of the events and sentiments of the people you met?

CORWIN: No, I fault myself for not having made more creative use of my opportunities. If you were to press me for exactly what creative opportunities, how those could have been improved, I would be hard pressed to answer. That would require, at this late stage, a whole new creative task.

BELL: A problem of putting together a radio documentary of that type was that you were facing linguistic obstacles and always working through interpreters. You were forced, when the actual voices were not speaking in English, to fade them under and go to an interpreter or your own synopsis of their words. Did you think that this might have blunted your presentation?

CORWIN: Not substantially, I don't think so. In terms of actual impact upon the listener, of course it's always better if your interviewee speaks in English. Thus, I was very lucky to have Nehru speaking in elegant English, but not so happy about having Chou En-Lai in China speaking in Chinese and then being faded down under an interpreter. It was not that I worried about the translation being accurate because usually there was no attempt made to dissemble or cover up. Actually, one of the areas of my discontent about *One World Flight* was that thirteen half-hours didn't begin to touch it. The substance of it was much broader than could be accommodated in that time. Were it today, in television, it would be thirteen hours which would double the length. Even in radio it would be that long because twenty-nine minutes and thirty seconds, less the opening and closing formats, cuts you down pretty much. To cover a country in twenty-six minutes and fifteen seconds net, doesn't give you much latitude. It certainly doesn't take into account that some people have a slow pattern of speech, and that there was the necessity of having to move in and out of their own languages.

BELL: I found much of it very inspiring. The man-in-the-street stuff, particularly, was very striking. But there seemed to be this incredible suspension at the time — bafflement, a holding of breath — regarding the prospects of world peace. Not that there didn't seem to be hope, but that the actual processes weren't even conceived of, except that the United States would have to take the lead. Did you feel that you were hearing the same thing over and over again?

CORWIN: No. There were quite sharp differences in the political and social climates of countries to which I went.

For example, the difference between Poland and Sweden or between Sweden and New Zealand were very, very marked. I didn't find that it was a one-tune experience at all.

BELL: Certainly the Poland-Sweden show was very good, and the Czechoslovakian show should certainly be heard again somehow, if only for the pathos. Have you thought of floating the idea to CBS Radio again that you, or someone else, should try this concept again and see what happens?

CORWIN: No, I haven't, and I appreciate your asking that question. In so doing you extend what I already appreciate as a seal of approval on this enterprise to begin with. I am encouraged to hear that you found some of the scripts and the people-on-the-street interviews moving. That gives me a better estimate of what I did. Maybe I'm too introverted about my memory of the whole experience.

But I'm cynical about any radio entity undertaking this now — unless it were to be foreign, unless it were to be the BBC — because American radio is simply not interested in that sort of thing, and they wouldn't put up the bucks. It costs money to travel; it costs money to be lodged; it costs money to edit — and nowhere in the entire spectrum of American radio is that to be found. Certainly not in Public Radio where you would look for it first. After what happened to NPR in the Mankiewicz disaster — I don't even want to attach it to his name because I greatly respect Frank Mankiewicz — they aren't going to spend that kind of money after such recent heavy losses.

BELL: There doesn't seem to be any one entity that would fund it, unless you could get an agreement to broadcast from one and funds from another.

CORWIN: Yes, it would have to be endowed. It would have to be a foundation or a whole series of foundations. I marvel that programs — such as Bill Moyers's one on secret government recently — get done at all.

BELL: What kind of a time lag was there between the last of your dramatic shows for CBS and the start of *One World Flight*?

CORWIN: There was never much of a time lag between one series and another. It was almost like chain-smoking. I was never conscious of having a breather of any extent. If I wasn't actually working on something, it was gearing up to work on it.

Thus, the time spent on writing and producing *One World Flight* was far longer than the months spent on the flight itself — getting visas and lining up the itinerary. I had to contact each of the CBS correspondents — in France, in England, in Egypt, in the Far East — and find out what it was possible to do and notify them when I would be there. It wasn't a case of going to see the Taj Mahal when I was in New Delhi. In fact, to this day I haven't seen the Taj Mahal. There wasn't time for that. Also, bear in mind that scheduling air flights was extremely difficult at that time because the domestic air service of many countries had been disrupted or destroyed by the war, so that there were many areas in the itinerary where there could not be advance bookings. It had to be done on unscheduled military planes. It was not easy.

Chapter 5

BELL: You were working on two projects at roughly the same time in 1942, both limited series — *This Is War!* and *An American in England.*

CORWIN: I didn't enjoy *This Is War!* which was a four-network show. Essentially it was an assembly-line procedure. It had to rely for its agenda and its information upon government bureaus and offices, the Navy Department and the State Department, the office of this and the bureau of that. It was a propagandistic enterprise, though on the right side to be sure.

There was some good writing in it. I wrote only about half the series, not all. We had some pretty damn good writers like Stephen Vincent Benét. That series developed Ranald McDougall, by the way. He was a page or something equally lowly at NBC, and he asked if he could write one of the programs. I liked it very much, recommended that it be done, and it was done. A great coup for a young writer to find his first work on a four-network broadcast.

BELL: *This Is War!* was a thirteen-week series, of which you directed twelve but only wrote six: "*America at War, It's in the Works, The Enemy, Concerning Axis Propaganda, To the Young,* and *Yours Received and Contents Noted,*" which concerned the correspondence that the series had received.

CORWIN: I think *To the Young* was a good one. They were not bad, as I reconstitute them in my mind, but they were not programs about which I can now get excited.

BELL: When you directed the scripts of some of the eminent names in literature involved with this series, were they content to hand their work over without many suggestions or reservations?

CORWIN: There was never a fuss. Most of those engaged, like Maxwell Anderson and Stephen Vincent Benét, knew very little about radio and were very tentative — a little bit scared of the medium — simply because of their lack of familiarity with it. They trusted me.

I directed all but one, which came from the coast at a time when I couldn't be there. *This Is War!* and a series called *So This Is Radio* are among the programs that I cheerfully forget. They weren't bad, but —

BELL: What was *So This Is Radio*?

CORWIN: That was a series inspired by my play, *Seems Radio Is Here to Stay*. Bill Lewis and everyone who had anything to do with it were so taken with that program that they got a little greedy and thought they could make a series in which radio was presented in the way that it was done in that play.

Again, it was kind of a PR job. I never have enjoyed that role and avoided it thereafter.

BELL: Might these things sound better to you today than they did then?

CORWIN: Possibly. One of my programs that I not only disliked, but had contempt for, was analyzed in the course of a doctoral thesis on my work by a scholar at the University of Oregon. In passing, he referred to this script and its virtues. His thesis gave me a little more respect for the script than I had had, but of course that was after many years.

There are certain programs that I have an aversion to. I never play them. Another in this category was a very big one, quite good in its concept and execution, called *Word from the People*. That was a biggie, drawing upon all of the continents — except Antarctica I guess — by shortwave, live.

BELL: Was that an assigned project?

CORWIN: No, I proposed it. Look, I've made mistakes, and I think that was one of them. It wasn't a serious mistake. I know a lot of people who liked it.

BELL: It's a good idea.

CORWIN: It was, but somehow, to me, there's another assembly-line quality about this piece. The guts of it was logistics, I felt.

Word from the People was a program that, as I say, I proposed. It was close to the end of the war. I wrote a memorandum in which I said that its objective would be to heighten public interest in the United Nations Conference in San Francisco in April of 1945.

I had high ideals for the program. I wanted it to express the hopes resident in all peoples, the simple and basic hopes for peace, freedom, and an international organization that would secure the world against wars in 1965, 1990,

2015, and points in between — on the basis that this was the current interval between serious wars.

The conference marked the inauguration of an unprecedented diplomatic Olympic Games, and I wanted to create a new kind of broadcast synthesizing reportage and showmanship.

Well, CBS went along. I was pretty much listened to at that time and quite occupied since the air dates of *Word from the People* and *On a Note of Triumph* were just a few days apart.

It was unrelenting hard work, much assisted by Charles Lewin and a capable staff. It was done in San Francisco with an all-star civilian cast — as opposed to the stars of show biz — except that I insisted that my principal voice, my narrator, be a total unknown. I wanted to get a man from the services, so I had CBS stations around the country look for him. They interviewed people according to my specifications, and they sent me tapes of the interviews.

One man stood out from all the rest — Harry Jackson from Pitchfork, Wyoming. You couldn't ask for a better dateline than that, could you? Harry had a very macho kind of voice and quality. He was intelligent. He was an infantryman, and he had been wounded. I think he was a sergeant. But around him on the show was an extraordinary battery of people. First of all, I wanted the program to come from all continents — live, shortwave. It was very, very involved. And since shortwave, then as now, is at the mercy of atmospheric conditions, we wanted protection against failure. So we transmitted program elements in advance of the actual broadcast and had standby recordings in case of trouble. This worked out. We had to resort to backup material in three or four instances. But there were pickups from Guam and Moscow and from Europe, of course, and from Australia.

Here's a scrapbook on this program which is just chock-full of cablegrams and telegrams and communications and budgets and autographs. It's incredible.

Here's a telegram from Thomas Mann, who was on the program, and one from Carl Sandburg. Here's one to Lew Wasserman. Here's one from Adlai Stevenson, whom Western Union insisted upon calling "Adelaide" Stevenson. He was then Assistant Secretary of State. And Secretary of State Stettinius was on the program. And Archibald MacLeish. And here's a telegram from a dragon of the period, Harry Cohn.

It was a sprawling, big, involved program. I have not listened to it once since it was done. I did not like it. It was not a bad show; it was a good show; and it got good ratings. But I guess a creator's feeling about a work is like a man's feelings about a woman — it's a matter of chemistry and attraction. Somehow, the vast amount of prefabrication bothered me in the final analysis. It seemed to me something put together in a factory rather than the kind of crafted, original, creative work that I considered my best.

BELL: Is that why you don't care for your *One World Flight* programs?

CORWIN: Well, that's a different set of concerns. I must say that I'm not altogether negative about the *One World Flight* programs. I just feel that I would like to have been sharper in the choice of questions that I asked the interviewees.

I have to be honest with you. I had favorites, and I had un-favorites. The difference being that I have listened to certain programs in the *One World Flight* series, and I've never listened to *Word from the People*. I wanted something of the sweep of the old *Empire* broadcasts of the BBC in that program. Those were stunning programs, and they arrested me. This one had the same sweep, and it also had meaning. It was really designed as a prologue to the United Nations conference, an unofficial prologue with the very best of intentions.

BELL: Could you say that the series *Transatlantic Call* was *your* series?

CORWIN: It began as my series. I became ill. I did three programs for that series. One was *New England*; another was about the Midwest; and the third one dealt with Washington, D.C. I had been in poor health and went to Chicago to do the program about the Midwest. A man named Stanley Merkin was my research assistant on that program and worked with me closely. We had all our meals together in the dining car, and he had a fearful cold. It was the dead of winter, and Chicago itself had a fearful cold. I caught a bad sore throat that quickly moved on to infect my ears, and I had the medically absurd condition of abscesses in both ears.

I came back to New York quite ill. This was just before penicillin came on the market, and it was the kind of condition that could last long and could recur. My doctor somehow liberated some penicillin for me but forbade me to go back to work and suggested that I fly off to some sunny climate and dry out, which I did. But to get to the series, it *was* a transatlantic call. The programs alternated, originating in London and in the States.

BELL: Was that your idea?

CORWIN: I think that it was brought to me. It was a good idea.

I thought two of my three programs were inferior by my standards. The third, however, was one of the best I ever put my hand to, and that was the program about the Midwest called *Midwest: Breadbasket and Arsenal*. It had a poetic stance. The flavor of it is established very quickly by the opening narration. Let me just read that opening to you.

"A few weeks from now, when spring pushes in from the Gulf of Mexico, moving upstream on the Mississippi, and fanning out over the flatlands — do you know what will happen? There will be a swinging open of barn doors on hinges that have just been oiled, and out of the barns onto the sweeping prairie will roll a million tractors ready for the earth. Not a poet's million, like a million stars, but a farmer's million, exactly 1,012,677 tractors all rolling out onto the plains, the continuous and gently tilting plains of the thirteen states known to the world, and to themselves, as the Middle West."

So, you see, that script had a kind of texture right from the start. I feel it's a good model for students because it took radio's ubiquity — its ability to leap distances — and used it well. It was simple in structure but at the same time was graphic for the people of Britain for whom it was intended. It was also informative for the domestic listener, because to give an idea of the scope of the Middle West, I had arranged to have commentators speaking live from the tops of the tallest buildings in the Middle West. I'll just give you the cues to show how this zipped around the landscape.

"From Chicago north and west as the crack trains fly, 450 miles in a direction which would eventually land you in Alaska, we take you now over rich dairy land, still covered by snow, over frozen rivers and forests of pine, to a city on the shores of Minnesota. Come in, city of Duluth.

"Voice: This is Ruth Lang Johnson, speaking from the top of a skyscraper in downtown Duluth. I'm looking out on the extreme western end of Lake Superior, biggest body of fresh water in the world, a lake so big it has a three-inch tide, so big that it could accommodate all of Denmark and Holland."

That immediately gave it some reference point for the British listener. Then she said, at the end of her bit:

"When the ice breaks, some of these freighters will clear for Cleveland, Ohio — another Midwestern city, 833 nautical miles distant. If you'll hold tight, Britain, we'll take you there now. Come in, Cleveland.

"Voice: This is Lawrence Demming, broadcasting from a building fifty-two stories above the streets of Cleveland, a city which is bigger than Athens, Greece."

He turned it over to Detroit, where George Cushing spoke from a point twenty-eight stories above the streets of a city that is bigger than Rome. Then we went to St. Louis, and Lambert Chiman broadcast from atop a twenty-story building. It kept going around like that. I wrote the text for all of these people, of course, based on the descriptive detail furnished me. There were many participants. In preparing the program, I had called the stations and asked them to have some of the announcers on their staff cut recordings for me, and I would pick from among them. George Cushing, in Detroit, was a typical voice. There were announcers on the staff who had great, rich, rolling voices; and George, not an announcer, happened to wander by the studio and thought, "Well, I'll go in and try it." He sounded like a regular guy, so I picked him. He told me later that his colleagues said, "My God, he picked *Cushing*? That's weird!"

BELL: You did more of those kinds of broadcasts than anybody, doing a dramatic broadcast from a variety of locations, live, using the lay of the land as a strand of character.   Did those programs inform your more conventionally designed dramas?

CORWIN: What was constantly in mind was almost congenital in terms of my birth in radio — a sense of delight in the space-annihilating properties of broadcasting. What better medium, then, to take you instantly from tower to tower, each a thousand miles apart, and describe the varieties of landscape. Glorious. I again used that technique in *Could Be* — where we go to imaginary areas of the world, zip-zapping from Paris to New Zealand and onward.

BELL: The *One World Flight* material was more sequential.

CORWIN: Sequential and personal.

BELL: Did you work on more than one script at a time on *26 by Corwin* for instance?

CORWIN: No, one script at a time. But I took notes toward others.

BELL: How far before the program did the first rehearsal take place?

CORWIN: The day of the broadcast. Only on one instance did a rehearsal extend to more than one day, and that was only because of external events. I refer to *On a Note of Triumph.*
　You may recall that there was a false armistice, a false report, and because it was false we suspended our preparations. I made a recording of the rehearsal, then went home, made some changes, and we resumed rehearsal the

next day. But always the rehearsal was on the very same day, right up to air time, beginning about six hours before.

BELL: Did you love that? Or did you hate it? It doesn't seem a situation that you can be neutral about.

CORWIN: When you have no other reference than that, you accept it. I didn't hate it. There were times when I felt that I would like more time, but we were accustomed to that kind of pressure.

It was an economic matter. We used live music, and if we got into overtime, it was a very costly business. My programs were never commercially sponsored, so cost was a big factor. We didn't have Campbell's Soup to lean on.

BELL: In the *Bill of Rights Show*, Bannerman mentions that you had a solo session for Jimmy Stewart before his work as the narrator in that broadcast. Did you do that often?

CORWIN: No, usually it was ensemble, no separation. I think, in the case of Stewart, it may have been because he had a very tight schedule, came in a little later than the others, and this was catch-up. I don't vividly recall that event.

BELL: Was it very difficult to assemble these casts?

CORWIN: I had a good right-hand man named Charles Lewin who was associated with me on many of these broadcasts. He knew a good many of the stars and had a very winning manner, like an agent with whom one feels comfortable. I have to say that I myself had a good name among these stars at that time, and some volunteered to be on programs. They would meet me socially and say, "By the way, I listen to your work, and anytime you write something in which I could be of help to you . . . ." Naturally, I seized on that.

BELL: Did you then proceed to write parts for them?

CORWIN: No, I never did. I just let them know when I had a part. I wrote the parts first and then cast them, except in certain cases such as Robert Young who went through as a character in a series, that being *Passport for Adams*. Then I would write for the character, but this was rare for me. On other occasions — such as a comedy for Ruth Gordon and various things for Charles Laughton and Elsa Lanchester — I might write for a friend.

For example, *Untitled* was not written for Freddie March. He was in New York and was kind enough to do it. I would say that maybe fifteen percent of my things were written for someone.

BELL: There was a segment in a program called *Cresta Blanca Carnival*, for the Mutual network, entitled *A Program to Be Opened in a Hundred Years*. Was this the only script produced for a network other than CBS, during the time you were there?

CORWIN: Yes, and I believe it was the only commercial program that I ever did.

BELL: Did you have to clear this with CBS?

CORWIN: Probably, but it was a small matter, and my contract did not stipulate exclusivity. I was frequently on programs on other networks as a guest. I did a *Fred Allen Program*. Fred did *My Client Curley*, and another time I was one of his guests, and he interviewed me — a typical, funny Allen script. I was in the alley.

BELL: Let's discuss technique. Did you prefer that actors mark their scripts for pacing and cues?

CORWIN: Whatever was comfortable for them. I've even had occasion where actors memorized their scripts.

BELL: Was there a patent method of page turning in radio, so they wouldn't sound on the air?

CORWIN: Just a matter of delicate handling, being careful.

BELL: Did you use a unidirectional mike, generally?

CORWIN: It depended on the script requirements. If you wanted to exclude extraneous sounds, to isolate, you used a unidirectional. Other times you needed one that was circumambient, non-directional.

Speaking of distractions, like rattling pages, there is something in radio to this day that I cannot stand which drives me up a wall. It's extremely sloppy on the part of both the actor and director. You'll hear it on commercials where somebody reads, comes to the end of a line, and then does a sharp intake of breath — and you hear the intake.

It's disturbing; it's untidy; it's easily gotten around by editing tape. You don't have to suck in your breath that hard. You can dispense with that sound.

BELL: How did movie actors adapt to the faster pace of radio?

CORWIN: It didn't seem to cause many problems for people who came from other media. There might have been a moment, a short period of adjustment, but it never seemed to be a problem, not in my experience.

BELL: And men like Martin Gabel or House Jameson — could they aspirate, respirate, for long periods? Did you have to worry about how sustained you were on them?

CORWIN: That was never a problem.

After all I've said about attention span, it may seem inconsistent to say that I was at some pains not to tax the patience of the listener with too much of the same color, not to be monotonous. I made more, I think, of the mosaic structure for that reason. I was careful not to bog down. There were times when the single voice took over, but usually that was justified by emotion or circumstance.

BELL: Well, your scripts have far more words per line, as it were, than just about any other in radio.

CORWIN: Perhaps so, but my reliance there was on the intrinsic interest in what was being said. You know and I know that there are speakers who are so compelling and satisfying that an hour's speech sometimes seems short. On the other hand, there are those who tire you out in forty seconds.

It depends on what is said; and perhaps I pushed that sometimes — I won't say to a limit — but I was unafraid to give Apollo a good, long farewell speech in *Descent of the Gods*; and I also gave full play to speakers who had something to say in *Could Be*, like the ones I've just quoted. They might go on for a minute or a minute and a quarter. I never felt I was losing my audience.

BELL: Was there ever any censorship of your subject matter from the brass at CBS? Gentle suggestions that a program might be a mistake?

CORWIN: No, never.

On one of the earliest shows, *Radio Primer*, Bill Lewis sent me a memo saying that he had enjoyed the show but thought it was something that would be appreciated mostly by the trade, that it was an inside joke. That view was not shared by the commentators. The reviewers liked that show. I was never stopped on any script.

BELL: What is the value of the intimate, small story today?

CORWIN: The intimate can be very important. Drama is present in the monologue — sometimes, it can be said, *especially* in a monologue — as in Chekhov's *Evils of Tobacco*, a marvelous work for solo performer.

I hope I have not been confusing about my allusion to intimacy; indeed one of my criticisms of television today is that it seems to have no patience with unsupported speech. So many directors feel that since it's a visual medium, the camera has to be making 360-degree orbits around the speaker. It's reflected in television commercials when the spokesman for the product is on the move, first word to last. They are very nervous that the *child* out in the audience there, that composite fourteen-year-old, will wander away from the set if anyone sits or stands still for a minute on end.

BELL: Does the slickness of TV commercials today bother you?

CORWIN: I often find slickness to be empty and boring. In a way it corresponds to the person who, out of insecurity because he feels there isn't much to himself or herself, affects eccentricities of dress, airs, and manners. That pertains in television to a great extent.

BELL: You are a co-winner of the first prize in the Metropolitan Opera Company Award for New American Opera for *The Warrior*, produced in 1947.

CORWIN: One day I received a letter from Bernard Rogers of the faculty of the Eastman School of Music. He said he wanted to write a one-act opera and that he was a follower of my work and wondered whether I would be willing to let him base an opera on some text of mine.

It is not every Tuesday that I get such a letter. I was flattered that someone wanted to devote his talent and time to writing music to go with my words — with any words of mine. I responded favorably. I told him to take his pick.

He wrote back to say that he would like to base an opera on one of my "Old Testament Trilogy" programs, *Samson*. I wrote back to suggest that there was already a very good opera by Saint-Saëns called *Samson and Delilah* and that he choose another. This did not brook him. He said there was enough room for another opera on Samson. I didn't argue with him further and wished him good luck.

He wrote the opera. It took him a year or so. I had completely forgotten about it when one day in New York, I got a call saying that he was in town, that he had the complete score and would like to show it to me. Well, I don't read scores with any particular training, but I invited him to come over because I wanted to meet him. He was a charming man, very gentle. He showed me the score, of which I feigned understanding, and again wished him good luck with it.

Not long after that meeting, he called with considerable enthusiasm to report that the League of Modern Composers had arranged for the opera to be done on a program at 11:30p.m. one night soon on CBS. It was to be in the charge of Bernard Herrmann, the conductor.

The day of the rehearsal arrived, and I was invited to attend. My wife and I went to a little studio around the corner from 485 Madison on 53rd Street. There were gathered Regina Resnick, Mac Harrell, and other worthies of the opera world. They started rehearsing the music, which was severely atonal.

This dismayed me. I have nothing against atonal music, but the text was Old Testamentary and sultry and had exhalations of the desert. It was about passion and lust and brute strength. The music, on the other hand, was mathematical and cool. Still, I was hearing only a piano reduction. I felt I must not allow my prejudices to get in the way, but Bernard Herrmann allowed his to do just that.

This was a morning rehearsal, so we went to lunch — to Louis and Armand's, the official restaurant of CBS — and there, in the presence of my wife Katherine and Bernard Rogers and his wife Betty, Herrmann proceeded to insult the work. He was so nasty that he succeeded in upsetting Rogers. I had been neutral since I was going so fast and had so many tasks swimming around — deadlines and things to do — that the loss of *Samson* as an opera would have no impact on my career or on me. But I was sympathetic to all the hard work Rogers had put in, and I wanted him to have at least a fair trial. The upshot was that the broadcast was canceled. Rogers was understandably hurt and bitter at Herrmann.

He called me sometime later and asked whether, since there was an element of disgrace attached to the episode, he could change the name of the opera. Poor Rogers, I thought. He should do anything he wants; I only hope he gets some measure of comfort out of whatever happens to this work from here on in. Sure, sure, change it.

He changed it to *The Warrior*, not a title that thrilled me, but he could have called it *Madame X* if he wanted. He called me sometime later and said that he was submitting *The Warrior* to the Alice M. Ditson Fund contest which was run by the Metropolitan Opera. Under the terms of the contest, it was to be submitted anonymously.

A year later I happened to be visiting my parents north of Boston when I got a phone call from my brother Al who was staying at my apartment on Central Park South. He told me I had a telegram from Edward Johnson, manager of the Metropolitan Opera, saying that I'd won an award. The wire didn't explain what it was for. I said, "Al, this is a mistake. It must have been meant for Norman Cordon." Cordon was then a well-known singer, and every now and then my name would be confused with his, as it was all the time with Norman Cousins.

"Call Johnson's office at the Met," I told Al. As I was saying that, it occurred to me that perhaps this was the opera by Rogers.

The award meant automatic production by the Metropolitan. It was given a lot of fanfare. ASCAP gave a big reception for Rogers and me, attended by Schumann-Heink and Jeritza and all the rest of them. Then came the opera itself which was broadcast in tandem with another since it was a one-act piece — it shared the bill with *Hansel and Gretel*.

BELL: Did you like it, ultimately?

CORWIN: No. It had a wonderful overture and then proceeded to go downhill into what seemed to me a maze of mathematical abstraction. It was savaged by all of the critics except one. It was liked by the critic for *The New Yorker*. Olin Downes in the *New York Times* attacked the opera not once, but on three Sundays running. I think *The Warrior* had two more performances and then disappeared from the repertoire.

Chapter 6

BELL: There are some wonderful things in *Thirteen for Corwin*, but I was particularly interested in Richard Goggin's essay about CBS from 1937 to 1943, painting it in the same light that you do.

I wanted to ask about a few people that he mentions.

Bill Lewis, I believe, we've already spoken about, but tell me more about Douglas Coulter. He later went into independent television production, is that right?

CORWIN: I don't know what Doug did in his last years. He and Lewis were the two principal figures in the program department when I got there. Coulter was in on the first interview that I had with Lewis. In a sense it was Coulter *and* Lewis who hired me. I was looking over some material the other day, and there were memoranda to and from Coulter. I recall that I got a telegram from Davidson Taylor after the first program of *Passport for Adams*, a series that I did starring Robert Young. Taylor wrote that Coulter had cried at three spots in the first program, which surprised me because I thought the program didn't have much in the way of emotion. I established the characters. In the script, Robert Young, playing the role of Doug Adams, is invited by a syndicate to go on this trip because he represents small-town American journalism. He has a leave-taking dinner with the family, with Harry Davenport as the grandfather. A quiet little program.

To get back to Coulter, he was a kind of a big bear of a man with a soft heart.

BELL: Was he complementary in personality to Bill Lewis?

CORWIN: No, Bill was a much more scintillating kind of man — bright and smiling and alert and charismatic — whereas Coulter was built like a tackle and had a deceptively gruff exterior.

The only thing that I ever had against him was when — in the absence of Bill Lewis and at the conclusion of *26 by Corwin* — he said there was no plan to continue with my kind of program. I was let go.

BELL: You actually went off the payroll?

CORWIN: I was off the payroll, but not for long, I must say. Lewis, within a matter of a few days, offered the *Bill of Rights Program* to me. When I told my agent — Nat Wolff — what had happened, he laughed. There was never a question of my being unemployable or unemployed for very long. I never went after Coulter to find out why — whether it was his hunch, whether there was a decision to economize. Both before and subsequent to that, Doug Coulter was very friendly. Indeed, I believe it was Coulter who strongly felt that I should do *On a Note of Triumph*. I think the assignment came from him. That alone would upset any notion that he was a heavy.

BELL: Was the war responsible for the prolongation of your kind of program, the suspension of commercial considerations for the duration?

CORWIN: Mark you, I was never troubled by CBS about considerations of what would be commercial. It never entered my thinking and only once entered the thinking of Bill Lewis when he voiced his concern to me that *Radio Primer* might have been too much "for the trade." In my conversation with William Paley on the eastbound *Chief,* after the war, he spoke to me of the need to reach as many radio sets as we could. But that came late in the day. It was never a factor in the work that I did subsequently. My heyday in radio was, by that time, past.

BELL: I was going to ask you about that conversation, which was reported in the Bannerman book. It seems to be one of those times and situations that should be sunk in amber, one of those end-of-paragraph sort of experiences.

CORWIN: Curious that you should speak of its special place in my log because in the autobiography that I began to write, commissioned by a publisher some fifteen or twenty years ago, I opened with that conversation. It was important punctuation, not only in my life, but in the history of broadcasting itself. The conversation reflected the change.
   Would it help if I read to you those pages?

BELL: That would be great.

CORWIN: This is the opening of the unpublished autobiography, the writing of which I suspended some years ago with the idea that I would one day get back to it. I may someday do that, although the opportunities grow shorter with each passing day. Anyway, here's how it opens.
   "The train rocked and swayed and jittered as it gobbled up an Arizona flat. I sat at a dirty window, chin on fist, and

moped. Night was one station down the line; God was in his heaven; Paley was two cars forward; but where the hell was I?

"Twilight is a sad time mostly to the romantically young. When you pass thirty-five, you are more likely to be glad for the eraser that wipes the board clean of the scribbling-and-chalk dust of the day. Except when you're already in gloom, dusk deepens and confirms and indulges it.

"So it was with me on that July evening in my thirty-eighth year, aboard the eastbound *Chief*, alone. All the mistakes I had ever made, and there were congresses of them, reeled past me like the darkening countryside — the resolves aborted; opportunities missed; works released too soon; scripts, speeches, words irrevocably printed or spoken; blunders in my personal life; stupidities; obstinacies; neglects of education; impetuous decisions; excesses of brashness and caution — all came together like a tweedy TV pattern, blurred and blobbed, a hail of dried bird shit. I tried to wallow up out of the slough, but a prescience lay heavy on me, an unparticularized hunch that there were dirty days ahead. Not disaster, necessarily, but embattlement, with a good chance that it would be on many fronts. Already it had begun, already I was beset by myself, and I was sure that others would be along to join. Behind me lay a crowded and coruscating world. Ahead, I felt, an emptying room.

"In that hour on the Santa Fe, nothing to which I had ever put my hand seemed much good. I reached for any kind of buttressing argument. Had I not, I asked myself, done better than just pull my own weight? Were there not works, praises, prizes, far travels, very important people? All hollow tokens, said the prosecutor inside me, all an index of circumstances and names and not a measure of myself. If I really had resources, I would not need to fumble over beads. I kept on trying to whistle in the gloaming. It did not help.

"It was like trying to console one freshly bereaved. The unreproachable good deeds of the deceased and his badges of merit are of cold cheer while the stiff lies in the next room. In this case the corpus was not quite dead, but so close to dying as to suggest the practicality of funeral arrangements. The name of the doomed was Radio, my first love — still rich, still big, but in the terminal phase of the wasting disease that was to end its usefulness as a medium for any serious artist.

"It was not the imminent end of radio that had me in the muck. It was myself. Yet my awareness that the passing of a craft that had been peculiarly my oyster, that I had helped develop, was not exactly therapeutic. Neither, it turned out soon enough, was Mr. Paley who, with his new second wife, was two cars forward. We had met briefly when boarding the train in Pasadena, and he said that he and bride were going to take the next twelve hours catching up on sleep but that he wanted to get together with me on the following day. We did, at a table in the dining car.

"William S. Paley was then President of the Columbia Broadcasting System, as he had been for twenty years. At forty-seven he was trim, handsome, warm, and had reserves of instant charm. For ten of those twenty years, we had known each other, not at all closely, but a notch or two beyond the usual employer-employee relationship. In my early days at CBS, when Paley was still married to Dorothy Hart Hearst, both of them would, every now and then, drop into the control room of some broadcast I was directing just to watch and listen, and we would chat afterward. Once in a while they would give a party at their town house, and I would be invited, along with a few other CBS men whom the network had the good taste never to call its 'family' —

Edward R. Murrow, William Shirer, and Charles Collingwood among them.

"In England, during the war when I was shortwaving a series of broadcasts back to America, Paley came over for a visit to his London staff. One night, he and I drove together to an R.A.F. airdrome in Cambridgeshire to watch Stirling bombers take off for a raid of Wilhelmshaven. We waited six tense hours for their return. All the planes made it home safely. Since Paley and I were the only outsiders at the base that night, the airmen considered us lucky fetishes to have around and urged us to stay.

"There were other times, other meetings, telephone calls, letters, not frequent, always cordial. He spoke at the Waldorf-Astoria one night when I was given a public send-off on a flight around the world. He welcomed me back at the end of the trip. He was, in those days, the perfect model of enlightened top brass. He stayed out of the way, never tried to impose his opinions or philosophy on his network's reporters or writers, had no antic qualities like Howard Hughes, no Caesar complex like Harry Cohn, no truck with nepotism like a hundred doting others. He inflicted no interminable memoranda on his charges, like David O. Selznick. I liked him.

"In the last years of the war, Paley was away from New York most of the time as a colonel in the Psychological Warfare Department overseas. It was because he'd been abroad, he said by way of opening our discussion, that he had missed hearing *On a Note of Triumph*, a broadcast which had made a stir in the radio industry and in the country at large. I wondered why he had not listened to it in the three years since he'd been back from Europe, especially since his deputy, Paul Kesten, acting president of CBS, cabled him, 'You can be doubly proud of Corwin, of CBS, and of radio.' The broadcast was amply available on recordings, so there was no ritual involved in hearing it. But one does not chide the boss about such an oversight, if it can fairly be called that, not when you're his guest at dinner. He had always been friendly, and he might not have liked the broadcast had he heard it.

"Soon came confirmation of the hunches of the night before. 'You know,' said Paley, picking at his salad, 'you've done big things that are appreciated by us and by a special audience, but couldn't you write for a broader public? That's what we're going to need more and more. We've simply got to face up to the fact that we're in a commercial business, and it's getting tougher all the time. If our programs don't aim to reach as many of the ninety million radio sets in the country as we can possibly get to tune us in, why then we're not really making the best use of our talent, our time, and our equipment.'

"A different Paley. War and the competition of NBC had apparently changed his thinking. When I had first come to CBS ten years ago, the network reserved blocks of time every week for unsponsored programs that were created and produced by CBS under a parasol known as 'public service.' In a printed rate schedule — an accordion-folded breakdown of the broadcasting week that fit into every time-salesman's coat pocket — such programs were blocked in green, and the proud legend 'Reserved From Sale' super-imposed. The Sunday afternoon concerts of the New York Philharmonic were in this green zone and *School of the Air* and *Americans at Work* and the *Columbia Workshop* and so were my programs. The network, as its top men had told me more than once, wasn't interested in how my programs were rated, for the shows were never going to command majority audiences, and there was no thought of selling me to a sponsor. I was generally scheduled opposite Bob Hope, the highest-rated program on the air — not as a sacrifice, not as a bone thrown to dogs — but because all of us at CBS felt that Hope's and my audiences were mutually exclusive.

"The *mene* of the handwriting on my wall, as far as radio was concerned, was now spelled out in fresh ink in Paley's hand. I knew what 'broader public' meant. I knew that to set out with the express aim of 'reaching as many sets as possible' would mean studying to write soap opera or gags or programs of towering innocuousness. Just how I was to command that broader public, Paley left to me. He was simply describing the new look, and the look was through a glass darkly, even for him.

"'There's going to be a terrible wave of reaction in this country,' he went on, 'McCarthy and McCarran and the rest, investigations and volunteer bloodhounds. No place will be safe for a liberal. Why, I went to a board meeting on Wall Street a little while ago, and to my surprise and embarrassment, I found myself congratulated on all sides for getting rid of Bill Shirer. In the first place, I hadn't gotten rid of him — he was moved to a less favorable time and chose to quit in protest — but I certainly was not happy about his quitting and even less happy to be congratulated for it.'

"But there were consoling outlooks, too. 'Jack Benny is coming over to us,' Paley said without any inflection. The announcement had not yet been made in the press, though there had been trade rumors. Getting Benny away from NBC seemed like getting Quebec away from Canada, so fixed had he been for so long in the heaven of that then richer and bigger network. I congratulated Paley on Benny and a moment later on the disclosure, new to me, that LP records were soon to supersede the 78 r.p.m. disc, a development from which Columbia Records, a subsidiary of CBS, stood to profit nicely. The rest of the talk tapered down to current movies and plays and books. Had he read

The Naked and the Dead? He hadn't. There was a brandy, and
we went to our respective cars.

"I sat in the dark, looking at the lights of a hamlet
through a procession of trackside trees, lights flickering like
fireflies. Where the hell, indeed, was I? I had never written
a stage play, a movie, a novel, a short story. I was a radio
writer, a new species. But it was clear now that my outlet,
the far-flung and pervasive Columbia network, was no
longer a Champs Elysées down which I could walk, run, or
skip as I had done in the past. Moreover, the rumblings of
reaction had steadily been getting louder in the hustings
and had been heard by Paley himself. CBS was known as a
liberal network, I as a liberal writer, and now he had said
'no place is safe for liberals.'

"Next morning Paley came to my room and invited me to
join him and Mrs. Paley between trains at Chicago, on the
yacht of Les Atlass on Lake Michigan. Atlass was a CBS
vice-president, owner of station WBBM, and his yacht was a
war-surplus item which he had converted from a naval
vessel.

"We did not go very far out on the lake. The only sight
worth remarking was Mrs. Paley, a beauty, one of three
Graces descended from the Harvey Cushings of Boston. She
hardly opened her patrician mouth. With her dark eyes and
porcelain skin and noble mane and mien, she didn't have to
speak. But then nobody on board had much to say. It was
hot, and the air was still. We looked at the water and the
skyline and each other, ate sandwiches and drank scotch,
and it was time to turn back and make for the *20th Century
Limited*.

"The *Century* pulled out slowly and rode through a
jungle of freight cars. There, in a tangle of tracks, my
thoughts tangled again. The despondency of the previous
night returned, intensified, and again I had to whistle up a

recital to persuade myself that I was, or at least had been, of account to somebody. Years later, backstage at a cavernous theatre in Vancouver before the curtain went up on the opening night of a play I directed, my stage manager over-heard Raymond Massey whispering to himself as he paced up and down in the costume of Abraham Lincoln, 'Remember Ray, you're a great actor. You can do it. You're a great actor.' In the same way, I was telling myself *I* could do it because I had done it. But do what? I was on a train going east on no particular business, without portfolio, without a target, heading into reaction, feeling uninspired, worn from the pace, sorry for myself, certain of the death of my medium, dull from scotch, and unnecessary.

"We passed a long string of freight cars travelling in the same direction, such a long caravan and moving so spunkily, it took minutes to leave it behind. I was sorry to lose the homely company. I had known freight trains and yards, known them well. They were the cyclorama of my boyhood."

BELL: In Mr. Paley's implication — equating art, commercialism, and liberalism — was he making a rational case to you?

CORWIN: Yes, I understood him. I understood his position. I think, had I been in his place, I might have arrived at the same conclusion. Galahads don't survive very long in corporate America — or England or Scandinavia for that matter. He had been Galahad for as long as he comfortably could be, and there were economic realities that faced him. On the other hand, while I understood where he was coming from, I felt that, notwithstanding all pressures, CBS — even in its direst straits — could still afford programs like mine, a writer-director-producer like myself. No matter what the weather forecast portended, I would not make the difference between bankruptcy and prosperity — especially since he mixed his bad tidings with good ones. He had just pulled off a tremendous stunt in bringing Benny over, so I had mixed feelings. I understood him but was not particularly happy about the way I was melted down into the total picture. I always felt that I was an ingredient that did not mix very well with conventional programming.

BELL: How could he have accomplished the same thing better than he did?

CORWIN: I have to qualify my answer by saying that I never knew Paley to have a hand in initiating or suggesting programs. He certainly did not dictate, that I knew of. Lewis and Coulter were suggesting programs all the time. In a way it was a vote of confidence in me — implying that he could leave it up to me. But the tenor of what he was saying was clear. It wasn't as though he were laying down a deadline or any fixed parameters. He was just expressing a general outlook. He certainly was right about the imminence of the dark age. I guess he was also right from the standpoint of the president of the network. It was no longer a gentleman's club. War clubs were being used.

BELL: You used the pronoun "us" when you said that "those of us at CBS felt that Bob Hope and I had mutually exclusive audiences."

CORWIN: I felt that way. I didn't resent a situation about which other people felt that I'd been thrown to the dogs, being opposite Hope. It was commented upon, though hardly all the time. I was very lucky to attract an audience of people who would never even bother to make the comparison, who were not even aware that Bob Hope was opposite me because he didn't interest them. But in broadcasting, minority audiences are still vast.

BELL: As you tolled your mistakes, was it that difficult to trace the march of events as opposed to those that you could possibly have had an influence upon?

CORWIN: The conversation with Paley just did not help. I started out in a low mood. When I had a series before me — a task, a deadline — I never had time to be melancholy or introspective. I was dealing with the exigencies of the work ahead. There was sport and élan and fun in the mix. But I was without portfolio.

One of the most significant things about that meeting was that I knew then that I *would* not change, that I *would* not conform, tack to the prevailing wind. I never undertook a project with the dominant goal of reaching as many people as I could, not once.

BELL: Do you condemn those who do?

CORWIN: Not in the least, any more than I condemn those who make fertilizer or suits of polyester — any commodity that will sell well.

BELL: Some of your war programs were manifestly informational, indoctrinational. Weren't you obliged to reach the most people possible?

CORWIN: Yes, well, you always *hope* that you will reach a very big audience. You *hope* that your *Hamlet* will play to big crowds. Van Gogh painted in hope that he would make a sale, turn a profit. Nobody wants to write for himself or herself, unless you are Emily Dickinson, and I don't think that even she did.

BELL: I can appreciate the hope, but past that there must have been the intention, the consideration of accessibility in many of your programs. You have professed to be anti-obscurantist. Can't you extend that into saying that you were concerned about being obscure in your ratings as well?

CORWIN: You have just equated rating and writing, and I don't think that's what you want to do.

BELL: How does one go about conceiving something with a huge audience, big ratings in mind, as opposed to doing only the best you can?

CORWIN: It is possible. I certainly conceived of a very big audience when I was addressing myself to the *Bill of Rights Program*. I knew it would be on every station in the country, no competition, none whatever, big ratings. I must stand by the claim that I never deliberately wrote obscurely. If I am, or ever was, obscure in any thought or expression or action or motivation or element in my writing or direction, I was at fault to have been and would have to apologize for it. But there is a clear distinction between unwitting and deliberate obscurantism. I felt that there was nothing obscure even in those programs that departed from what might be called "generally assimilable." It's not a question of obscurity or lack of understanding that separates the high raters from the low raters. [The television series] *Cagney and Lacey* just got canceled yesterday. That was not a program that anyone had any trouble understanding. What it takes to get a rating is, sometimes, the kind of ingredient that we are all embarrassed by.

BELL: To quote Richard Goggin, most of the sponsored programs at CBS were produced by ad agencies, and they were not privy to the administrative problems and strategies of the 20th floor executives.

CORWIN: The one executive, outside of Lewis and Coulter, that I had the most contact with was Paul Kesten. He was acting president when the war came and Paley was made a Colonel in the OSS or some other branch of the Army. Paley was absent a good deal of the time and Kesten was CBS's president in his absence.

BELL: Had he come from within the organization?

CORWIN: Yes, he had, I think so.
      There is in the Bannerman biography a telegram that I got from Kesten after he heard *On a Note of Triumph*. A man could die happily after receiving a teletype of that nature. It was so beautifully complimentary. It was a measure of the man that he could phrase that kind of a text. I speak of cordiality, but that was more than cordial. Stanton was also very cordial. Paley, too.
      But the week-in week-out activity of a writer-producer-director such as myself prevented much contact with those people. They were satisfied with what I was doing, and they had high administrative functions, and those seldom engaged the program department unless something was wrong or something was very right.

BELL: Frank Stanton at this time was not the programming guru that he later became.

CORWIN: No, but he always had an eye and an ear alert for what was being done. Long before Frank became president, he expressed great interest in my work. Indeed, he called me on the phone one day and asked if I could drop in, and I did, and he said, "You know, your book, *Thirteen by Corwin*" — which had just been published — "we would like your publisher to print a special edition for us of a thousand copies. Would you be willing, in that event, to write a special foreword for us?"

I said, "You bet I would."

The edition was printed and sent out in a very attractive box. And the legend on the box was accompanied by photographs of six or seven books by men associated with CBS, including Ed Murrow and Bill Shirer and *Columbia Workshop* plays edited by Coulter. The legend was, "Thirteen by Corwin is Seven by CBS" or something like that.

Not only that, but they took out a double-spread color ad in *Fortune* magazine, which at that time was large-format like *Life*. That was Stanton's decision. I'm sure he was involved also in the decision to make a special printing of *Seems Radio Is Here to Stay*, which I don't think any network ever did before or since. It was extraordinary, their interest in reaching toward some form of expression that would approach art.

I think they felt that way about my writing. I know they felt it about MacLeish. I don't know how many others were favored by that kind of dispensation, but I certainly was a beneficiary of it.

BELL: You mentioned Shirer and Murrow. Did you have some kind of status as the favorite playwright of the news department?

CORWIN: Not as such, although key performing members of the news department, like Shirer and Murrow, were keenly aware of my work.

BELL: There is a sense now of Murrow being the archetype of the trench coat and the slouch hat and the microphone, a very romantic image. Was the CBS news department at that time quite full of itself?

CORWIN: Yes, they did have a good sense of themselves, but it was never, to my recollection, a stance. It was never an exercise in preening or vaunting or saying, "We're number one." They were damn good journalists, and they knew it. But they never bragged about it. There wasn't time. I think that most of those men were of such serious purport that there was little thought given to where they stood against the opposition. They knew they were better than the opposition, that the news department in its cumulative resources and effectiveness was superior. They were all good, earnest people, and gifted at what they were doing. Ed Murrow was very much honored in London, but it never went to his head.

BELL: Didn't he catch flak at one time, during and after the war, for courting the bigwigs?

CORWIN: Ed was never one to cultivate celebrities. They courted him. They were aware of his prestige in America and the respect with which he was regarded, not only by his own network but by all of radio and the listening public. So it was to their advantage to cultivate Ed's goodwill.
    He was, to a certain extent, a confidant of Churchill. He was, at the same time, a good friend of Harold Laski, certainly to the left of Mr. Churchill. He was the one

American in broadcasting who stood highest in the eyes of the British.

BELL: Do you believe, in retrospect, that he did better work on television?

CORWIN: I think the circumstances and the medium made him more influential on television since television is a more influential medium — too damn influential in many respects.

It was circumstances like the famous McCarthy broadcast that presented him with an historic proscenium upon which he could perform. There had been no opportunity quite like that in radio. But it was simply an accident of history. Had McCarthy flourished in the days before television, I'm sure Ed would have been just as effective in that medium. He would have made just as striking a broadcast.

BELL: He was a very good friend of yours?

CORWIN: He did me a great personal favor by writing a letter of endorsement when I applied to adopt my son. He certainly was more than helpful in the *American in England* series. In fact, he shared the producership of that with me. He was my associate producer. But I don't want to exaggerate the closeness of our friendship. We didn't see each other that often. Over the years there were exchanged between us a dozen to twenty letters, and we met socially — outside of London, where we met daily, working — maybe a total of a dozen or twenty times, again, at his home or at CBS functions. He gave a wedding party for Kate and myself. I continue to be in occasional touch with his widow, Janet. But it would be presumptuous of me to imply that I was a close friend. That's a special category. I would like to have been, but I was not.

BELL: You mentioned associate producership. Writer-producer-director Arch Oboler said that, in his eyes, being the producer of his own program meant mostly that there was that much less interference in what he was doing.

CORWIN: Well, Oboler's right. Any time a producer can hyphenate his bearing on a project, it's a tremendous time-saving device. Also, it's hassle-reducing.

The function of the producer in radio varied from producer to producer. I sometimes wrote or directed programs which were produced by others, and the degree to which the producer was involved in or tried to meddle with the content and style of a broadcast depended on the individual. Mostly, he represented the budgeting and stayed out of it. Now and then — as in the case of a man like Werner Michel, for whom I did a program after I left CBS — there was a friendly association, and I was always open to input from anyone whose judgment I respected.

BELL: Was there a producer at CBS during the time you were there who was particularly respected, or was there more or less a "producing unit"?

CORWIN: No. Most of the directors were their own producers as well.

My function was a bit enlarged because I was also a writer. But with men like Earle McGill and Brewster Morgan or a woman like Nila Mack — and to an extent Robert Shayon and Richard Sanville — mostly they were their own producers as well as directors.

The producer function was a natural one. It was not tacked on. In other words, you're a director, and you're told by Bill Lewis or Doug Coulter how much money you'll have for the show. You prorate that according to the requirements of the show, the number of weeks or whatever; and you hold auditions, cast it from your own knowledge of actors.

There was no producer riding herd over those things, saying, "All right, Sanville, who do you propose to cast in that?" That was up to him to make sure that the sound department and engineering department and so forth were coordinated into the action.

BELL: Another figure of the time who cast a large shadow then, and perhaps even a larger shadow now, was Bernard Herrmann. You definitely worked with him as much as anyone in radio.

CORWIN: Probably more.

BELL: He seems to be associated with Orson Welles in radio and Hitchcock in films. But you used him at least as much as either of those two, and we don't know much about him. What kind of a man was he?

CORWIN: He was a man of considerable temperament. Of all the collaborators I had in radio production — and by collaborators I mean also those who wrote or acted — I was closest to Herrmann. One time, when he found himself without lodgings in Los Angeles, I took him in when I was doing a series for CBS. I invited him to share an apartment I had at the Sunset Towers as my guest.

Later, my wife and I saw him through his divorce from his second wife. We spent a good many evenings together, dinners at his place or at ours or at restaurants. I got to know him well. He was a close friend. I spoke at the memorial service for him in Hollywood.

BELL: His music seems to have a kind of energy that lays below the surface, frequently bubbling to the surface in eruption. One would infer a quiet man with a short fuse.

CORWIN: He had a short fuse; he was shrill. He was extremely zealous about the composer's rightful function — or what he perceived as the composer's rightful function in a medium where music was mostly being used as an element of production rather than front and center as an independent element.

BELL: He was the kind of collaborator, then, who would say: "Give me more to do," or "Can I fit something under this dialogue?"

CORWIN: He was very resourceful, and I quickly learned to trust his judgment. I would tell him what my concept of the spirit of the music was and what my intention was, dramatically, and leave the rest up to him. Every now and then he would inform me of what he was about to do, and if I had any objection, I would make it. But I usually did not, and he always hit exactly the right note.

There was very little lead time in my productions, and I tended to use it up too soon. I would send Herrmann the pages that involved music, if not the entire script, because I generally worked on them right up to the deadline. Our work coincided. It wasn't as though I finished a script a month ahead, and he had time to work on it. I would phone him, usually explain the premise, concept, and action of the script — and the intended development — so that he was familiarized at least with the spirit as well as the scenario.

On one occasion we were crossing the country, and each of us had a compartment on the Santa Fe *Chief*. We were working on a script which I had adapted from many different sources in the writings of Thomas Wolfe. The pages, when I finished them, made a short transit from my compartment to his — as soon as they came out of my typewriter, he had them. He worked on the train, so that by the time we reached Los Angeles the score was finished. It turned out to be one of the finest scores anybody ever did for me, and I believe one of the finest ever written for the medium.

BELL: There was, interestingly, a program in the *26 by Corwin* series, according to the Bannerman biography, called *Wolfeiana*, on October 5, 1941. Then, down the line in the *Columbia Presents Corwin* series, there was a program called *Wolfe*. Was there any connection between the two?

CORWIN: *Wolfe* was a different program. They are similar in some ways, but the later program opens with a letter from Thomas Wolfe that was not in the first one. The score for *Wolfe* was by Bernard Herrmann, written on the *Chief*. The score for *Wolfeiana* was by Alexander Semmler.

BELL: So you did work from the earlier script for the *Wolfe* program with Herrmann?

CORWIN: I must have because there are elements common to both, especially the train sequences, but there are quite a lot of differences, too. The second program profited from the experience of the first. I knew what didn't work particularly well. The first was from New York, and the second was from Hollywood.

I have both of the scripts right here. Here's the calling of the states and the tribes of Indians — that was common to both. But they ended differently.

BELL: There seems to be much more pure narration in the second version.

CORWIN: Well, in the second I was taking advantage of Charles Laughton in the role.

In *Wolfe*, Herrmann and I integrated sound and music in a kind of close-knit relationship that was unusual. It took more of the form which, musically, you would call a rhapsody. And the music was background, too, and sometimes took over the narration from Laughton. The program had a lot of good things going for it.

BELL: What kind of sound elements are you talking about?

CORWIN: *Wolfe* made a great deal of trains, and I had a wonderful time working with my sound men — who also enjoyed it — on railroad sounds, on the switching yards, on freight trains, on passenger trains in flight. And we processed the sound so that it would give the listener the impression, conforming to Wolfe's words, of a train speeding up, slowing down, passing through stations, riding over bridges — which makes a quite different sound from riding on terra firma.

For a passage that began in a train depot — a great depot like Grand Central Station or one of the great Chicago depots — Herrmann began the passage with a series of marvelously contrived, spaced chords which accelerated in the pattern of a steam engine starting up. It sounds simple, but you have to hear it to appreciate its ingenuity.

My function was to blend and to balance these elements. I went from that special musical effect into sound. Once the acceleration reached a certain point, sound took over from music, and the two had a kind of reciprocal function over the course of the program. Sound and music would sometimes go together then one would slip away or the other would return, very often so smoothly that it approached being imperceptible.

Herrmann was a daring composer. He did not look upon himself as longhaired; indeed he had short hair and was forever tugging at it in a nervous gesture. He never thought of himself as an experimenter, as avant-garde. He bore the same relation to his musicianship as the newsmen I spoke about a while ago bore to their journalism. It was unpretentious. He was greatly gifted but did not go around flashing medals and ribbons to pronounce his uniqueness.

BELL: He's noted for his arrangements and instrumentation. Working closely with him, you must have had a sense of whether he was hearing trombones, then writing a melody that suited trombones, or writing the melody and then assigning the trombones later.

CORWIN: I think he thought first of the material that he was working with, what its requirements would be. Then I think he thought of the instrumentation and wrote for those instruments.

I should explain that CBS in its sustaining operations had something that no network now has, and that was a house orchestra which was capable of playing either classical or popular music. The number of available musicians, depending on the demand for the orchestra by other programs, varied from week to week. The house musicians didn't come out of the budget, but it wasn't every week that you could arrange for the whole orchestra or even a large part of it. You made advance reservations. You said, "A week from Sunday I would like to get an orchestra of at least thirty-five pieces." I think it may have gone up as high as fifty.

A definitive example of Herrmann's scoring was when I wrote what I called an "Old Testament Trilogy." The first was based on the Book of Judges and its story of Samson. Others had to do with Job and the Book of Esther.

I learned that on the week for *Samson*, I would have the full orchestra available. I called Herrmann with that good news, and he received it indifferently.

"Who wants a big orchestra? I've seen the script, and I think it should have a very sparse orchestra." I said, "Tell me what you have in mind."

"Sure," he said, "four harps, a piccolo, tympani, and a clarinet." I said, "That's very strange, but I find it exotic."

"You're right," he said, "the script is exotic."

"Go to it," I said. It turned out to be an extraordinarily effective score.

BELL: Then you had to hire three harps, outside of the house harpist.

CORWIN: Right.

BELL: Was the instrumentation similar for the Job and Esther stories?

CORWIN: No, he didn't do the score for *Esther* which was a little one-act opera. That score was written by Lyn Murray and was big-sized.

Herrmann also had an unusual instrumentation for *Untitled*. Again, very sparse.

His score for *On a Note of Triumph* was absolutely impeccable from my point of view. *Variety*, in reviewing that program, said that the music was to that production what a great shortstop is to a baseball team.

BELL: Do you regard yourself and Herrmann as a strange pairing?

CORWIN: Not at all. I felt very comfortable with him, and he with me. We were good friends.

But after he went to England, I didn't hear from him much. On his last return from England, I didn't even know he was in town. One does drift, especially if you are thousands of miles apart, so it was not a friendship which went on an even and continuous level.

BELL: What sort of a man is Lyn Murray?

CORWIN: He's represented in the bookstores by a recent journal of his called *The Musician*. I wrote the foreword to it.

Murray was the next closest of my associates in music and, I'm happy to say, long-lasting. We do see each other frequently, and I was instrumental in getting him to write that journal. I helped him in the editing of it and got him a publisher. We have a good relationship. Lyn is as extroverted and uncomplicated as Herrmann was the opposite.

Lyn did some big productions for me. I mentioned *Esther*. He scored *Document A/777*, a substantial United Nations program. He scored *The Long Name None Could Spell* which I count one of my better programs. I would say that he had almost as many collaborations with me as did Herrmann.

BELL: How would you characterize him as a musician?

CORWIN: Much more versatile than Herrmann in the sense that he had a very strong hand in choral music and could write with equal ease music for a passionate documentary such as *The Long Name None Could Spell* or a little biblical opera or a musical comedy. He did *Radio Primer*, of which I sometimes think his music was the best. part. In that show he did a setting of a piece I wrote called "The Variety Song" which is marvelously contrived. He went on to do quite a bit of work for movies and television, mostly television, including many of the *National Geographic* specials.

BELL: Who is Guy Della Cioppa?

CORWIN: He was a production assistant, later a director in his own right, and a writer. Guy is a man of great charm, the sort of bright, executive type who would attract the notice of a man like William S. Paley. Paley engaged him as a kind of aide. I felt that creative radio lost a great deal when Guy was siphoned off into the executive suite.

BELL: I was going to ask if he worked his way down from Paley's office into production, but it was the other way around.

CORWIN: Yes. And when that association ended, that is to say the "executive-right-hand" arrangement, he became a network vice-president and operated out of KNX here.

BELL: How long did that last?

CORWIN: Many years. I don't know what broke it up, but he's been in independent production for the last eight or ten years.

BELL: You worked with John Dietz?

CORWIN: Yes, John Dietz was an engineer.

BELL: Did you have a rotational system for engineers at CBS?

CORWIN: It wasn't consciously rotational. It was largely governed by who was on duty, and the schedule of the engineering department. Now and then, if there was some very special requirement, I would ask for a certain engineer, and I usually got him. They were all pretty good.

BELL: In retrospect, would you say that was a pretty rote job, not necessarily on your broadcasts, but on the average comedy or soap opera?

CORWIN: Yes, I would say it was rote, but I'm glad you made the exception because my shows were necessarily more complicated.

BELL: Did Bill Robson have other week-to-week tasks besides the *Columbia Workshop*?

CORWIN: I think he was not confined to the *Workshop*. I think he had some special programs. *Man Behind the Gun* was one of his, and there were others that I'm not too familiar with, but I know he was not simply confined to the *Workshop*.

The progression there — what in historical terms you could consider the succession of key directors — was Irving Reis, Bill Robson, and myself. Bill brought to the role of director a conscious panache which was not demonstrated by Irving Reis or myself. Bill has a theatrical personality, and I don't mean that in any pejorative sense. Bill is by nature a colorful man given to a good deal of self-expression in dress and his outlook. I say that admiringly.

I felt, especially since I was new at the network, that Bill had been there for a generation, though it wasn't very long. He seemed to have full knowledge of the ropes and how to pull them. He was at first paternalistic in his attitude toward me, helping this youngster along.

I think Bill may later have rued the day that he did because I took over what he had enjoyed — not because I surpassed him, but because he drifted toward commercial radio and relinquished the special relationship that a director exercised in producing programs for the *Columbia Workshop*.

Much later, on the order of perhaps twenty years later, I ran into Bill one day in Hollywood.

It was lunch time, and we went to a little Italian restaurant on Sunset and Gower. And among other things, he told me that in those moments that he was being generous in his praise of me — he kind of hated my guts for having stuck to the *Workshop* and done the work that he best enjoyed and felt he had a strong hold on.

I shouldn't use the phrase "hated my guts," but again, it was an act of great generosity and openness for him to tell me that it had disturbed him and that behind those compliments was a little regret, tinged with bitterness.

BELL: No doubt he made a little more coin out of radio than you did.

CORWIN: There are probably very few fellow workers of any consequence in radio that didn't make more coin than I did.

BELL: I trust you didn't really listen to much radio when you were writing it.

CORWIN: Didn't have time.

BELL: But you, no doubt, had to keep reading.

CORWIN: To a limited extent, the act of writing wiped out a great many things, including reading and socializing and dining and the taking of vacations and enjoying the company of my favorite sex, which is women. Lots of things that really kept me in a kind of monastic routine.

BELL: Then, after a certain point, conceptualizing a script — given that you were too busy to cast your net into the world of ideas — might have been as difficult as actually writing it?

CORWIN: Sometimes, yes, more difficult than writing.

BELL: So, not to downgrade the concepts at all, but were things like your American-writer trilogy or your biblical trilogy conceptual shortcuts? "I can write three scripts without having to agonize over three new ideas?"

CORWIN: I never thought of it that way, but now that you mention it, it's a good idea.

I didn't take the easy way out by adapting. I was drawn to that task by great enthusiasm for the works that I adapted. I was fascinated by the richness of language and concept in the Book of Job and the marvelously melodramatic trajectory of the Book of Esther, which has yet to be made into the great movie musical that it could be.

Samson was not an adaptation at all. *Samson* was original, and I took it on to see just what would come of my taking a familiar biblical story and trying to give it a new twist — a feminist twist. It is not one of my favorite scripts. I think I went overboard in certain places, although there are some good lines. *Theatre* magazine, a prestige publication, gave it very high marks.

As for the "American Writers Trilogy," the *Sandburg* and *Whitman* shows do not rank high in my list of achievements, but the *Wolfe* one does, and I'm very glad I did that because it brought out that score by Bernard Herrmann. It remains, to this day, one of my favorite pieces, and it turns out also to be one of Ray Bradbury's two favorite pieces of mine. This is a long answer to your question of whether the adaptations were an escape. They weren't.

BELL: Not necessarily that the adaptations were an escape, but that you could expand on the themes already there, rather than having to generate three concepts at the alternative cost of one.

CORWIN: Well, I'll tell you. Conceiving was not always painful. There is the analogy between fathering a child and adopting one. There's a good deal of pleasure in the fathering, at least momentarily.

Chapter 7

BELL: You mentioned that you left CBS over a contract dispute. Over money?

CORWIN: Yes, I resisted all of these seven-year contracts which were standard. I felt that I didn't want to be chained to anything for seven years.

BELL: Then you didn't sign one initially, in 1938?

CORWIN: I did, but I later cut it down to three years. All of my contracts were for three-year terms. The fourth of those contracts included a new clause to the effect that if there were any secondary use of material that I wrote for CBS — they wanted fifty percent of the proceeds.

There had been things of mine that had been used secondarily. One was *My Client Curley,* and there were offers such as *They Fly Through the Air* which could have become something. I felt the new clause was confiscatory, especially since my arrangement with CBS had been relaxed, from my point of view. I was a kind of Boy Scout — eager and in love with my work. I felt it so much a lucky break to be doing my thing on a great network to a vast audience — attended by a lot of attention, honors, and publicity. I didn't have an agent when I dealt with CBS. As a consequence of this, I was paid $100 per script. Of course by the time I did _On a Note of Triumph,_ I was getting much more, but I didn't even get paid for that as a script at all. That was part of my overall fee, a good one at that period, my annual salary.

BELL: You got paid a salary and per script.

CORWIN: Yes. But as I say, they paid me $100 for each script, which was laughable. While the network was very good to me in some respects, they were stingy, too.

BELL: If they were going to sign you to another three-year contract, you might have gotten to write television scripts and profited from subsidiary uses.

CORWIN: That comes under the heading of corporate chess games, and I never had any understanding of them or patience with them.

The contract dispute could have been due to any number of contributing factors — such as an eager-beaver contract lawyer who wanted to win chevrons from CBS. It could have been greed or any number of things.

I wrote a note to Stanton, who was and still is a good friend, and told him what I was doing when they offered me this contract. But nothing came of that. You see, I have to stop here and explain my reasoning on this. I was out here on the coast at the time, and I just stayed out here, didn't go back to New York. Parenthetically, I must say that I later did do some work for CBS

But my position then was that if I did a program for CBS that was good enough to attract outside interest and become a movie or be adapted to the theatre, this not only fulfilled my obligation to them — which was to deliver a good production — but indicated that I had gone beyond that. If they acted as an agent or negotiated for that secondary use, then they were entitled to an agent's commission and nothing more. I thought fifty percent was confiscatory.

So, I was sufficiently annoyed to say, "That's it."

BELL: Do you remember how they responded to that logic?

CORWIN: They didn't respond at all.

BELL: You had moved out here by the end of the war.

CORWIN: Yes. I bought a home in Los Angeles in 1948, near Studio City on a high hill overlooking what is now Universal City, south of Ventura. The last house — or the first house, wherever you want to begin — on Lankershim Boulevard. It runs up the hill briefly on a private road. That was my house.

BELL: At this time did you feel that you wanted to write instead of going back to radio?

CORWIN: Yes, and I did write movies.

BELL: Weren't the seven-year contracts for writers being phased out in the studios by this time?

CORWIN: Yes, and in radio as well. The imminence of the phasing out probably contributed to CBS's attitude. This is sheer speculation, but their thinking could have been that they didn't have much to lose in losing any of their radio people.

BELL: Did you have any offers to direct a movie out here at that time?

CORWIN: I had an offer from Edwin Knopf, a producer at Metro, but there was something in my situation then that precluded me from doing this because it was to be shot in France.

BELL: What was the script?

CORWIN: It was called *The Vintage*. It starred Mel Ferrer, Audrey Hepburn, and Michelle Morgan and was directed by Jeff Hayden.

BELL: Could you say a few words about your program for the United Nations, *Windows on the World*, which used the Secretariat Building itself as a matrix for the operations of the organization.

CORWIN: I started in the sub-sub-sub-basement of that gigantic monolith, the UN Secretariat Building, and went floor by floor to the very top, interviewing the people of many countries and cultures who made up the Secretariat. They described what they were doing, and it all came together as a lively, colorful, informative documentary — one of the best I produced as head of special projects for U.N. Radio.

BELL: Why were there such extended gaps between your last three programs for the UN?

CORWIN: I did not work full time with the UN because my home was in California, and I wanted to be with my family part of the year. I considered it to be a *pro bono publico* occupation to begin with because there was more money to be made out here in California than at the UN. I did *Document A/777* out here, the rest in New York.

BELL: Bannerman quotes you as favoring New York over California. Why did you settle here ultimately?

CORWIN: When you establish a home and family, you sink roots, even if you are transplanted. I sank those roots here. I got to enjoy California, and at the same time I became somewhat disenchanted with New York. For one thing, I could never forgive that city for permitting the death of its great newspapers. That a city of that size — with its wealth and educational facilities, with a reputation as the cultural center of America — should permit the *Herald-Tribune* and the *Sun* and the *Telegram* and the *World* to go down was unconscionable. Also, I felt that the city had overgrown sane boundaries.

BELL: Are you asked to contribute editorially to newspapers?

CORWIN: Not editorially, although occasionally I write pieces for the op-ed pages, especially for the *Los Angeles Times*. Also I write reviews. In recent years I've grown away from that because I have a sense of diminishing time options. It takes quite a while to read a book, if you're going to do it properly, and then to write the review. The return is poor.

BELL: You were asked to write book reviews?

CORWIN: Yes, and now and then something for the magazine section. Over the last twenty years, I have written twenty or thirty such pieces.

BELL: Your last program for U.N. Radio, four years after *Windows on the World*, was *The Charter in the Saucer*.

CORWIN: Yes, it was lighter in texture than my other UN specials, closer to the comedy-fantasies that I had occasionally done for CBS. It dealt with a lone space voyager who comes from a planet riddled with problems, including six sexes — *hlam, hlum, hlom, hlem, hlop,* and *gleux,* of which only members of the latter are permitted to vote — an overbearing religion based on worship of the Almighty Dramchee which was worth $.00006 U.S. at the time. The planet had vexing labor policies wherein the hardest workers are paid the least, and also paralyzing semantic difficulties — their *and* has forty-seven different meanings, their *but,* sixty-five. Numbers are so fraught with emotion that indigenes sometimes weep over a decimal point, and music on the planet is so bad that wars are fought for the right not to listen to it.

The script, while light in tone, had serious underpinnings. It was not produced in this country but in England with none other than Sir Laurence Olivier in the leading role. I was nowhere near the production and was not happy with the way it came out.

BELL: Why was the program done in England?

CORWIN: Because at this stage the American networks, which had hitherto donated facilities and technical personnel to UN productions, decided to tighten their belts and *charge* for these services. The BBC had no such change in policy.

BELL: Why didn't you go to England to take charge of this program as you had the others?

CORWIN: I had confidence that the BBC, which had long done distinguished work in radio, would do well by my script. It turned out I was wrong. You win some, and you lose some.

BELL: How did you get involved with the United Nations to begin with?

CORWIN: I was in England, doing the *American in England* series, and I met Gibson Parker who was then with the BBC. He later joined the Secretariat of the UN in the capacity of producer and general factotum of U.N. Radio.

Gibson knew that I had left CBS over a contract dispute and asked if I might be interested in creating a new portfolio.

Their name for the position they designated was Chief of Special Projects. That is indeed descriptive of my function. I was not in any way involved in the routine activity of that entity, but I did address myself to special occasions and special programs. These were broadcast by one or another of the American networks.

BELL: Was U.N. Radio projected to be a world broadcast entity of several languages, ultimately?

CORWIN: Yes, although that was not its primary function. It was dedicated largely to creating programs in English which later would be translated or done by companies in other countries from the script that was written by the UN.

BELL: The best-remembered of these programs is *Document A/777*.

CORWIN: That program commemorated the signing of the Universal Declaration of Human Rights, perhaps the most important document yet issued by the United Nations though not yet fully honored or even acknowledged. But the United States and many other countries are signatories to it, and we all, to a greater or lesser extent, ignore the existence of the document in principle.

I may add parenthetically that it is a far more sweeping document for human rights than the American Bill of Rights, though of course it is indebted to all of the documents of freedom that preceded it. It was called *Document A/777* for the Declaration's number in the United Nations files. I thought that the three sevens, in addition to being of interest to poker players, were singular enough to justify its use as a title. Document A *stroke* seven, seven, seven.

For an earlier program, the first in what has become an annual concert celebrating the Declaration, I negotiated with and got the agreement of Serge Koussevitsky, then the conductor of the Boston Symphony Orchestra, to lend that great orchestra. Koussevitsky himself was ill, and his doctor had forbidden him to go beyond the summer program at Tanglewood, Massachusetts. The concert was to be in December.

But he said to me, "I have a very bright, young conductor who will take over the orchestra for me, and I know you will be in good hands." That was Leonard Bernstein.

That concert was the first to be telecast from Carnegie Hall, and certain structural changes had to be made to accommodate our controls.

There is a preamble to the Universal Declaration of Human Rights, and it is short. A minute and twenty-five seconds perhaps, or two minutes, and we thought big. We asked Laurence Olivier if he would fly over from England to do it. He agreed.

Somebody in the Secretariat thought that maybe we could get an airline to chip in his passage. Olivier said that he would do it without fee, but he would not fly as the guest of an airline.

I wanted some music behind that text. Again, thinking big, I called Aaron Copland — whom I did know, had met a number of times — and told him about the occasion and said we could pay $500 for that one use and that he would retain ownership thereafter. He agreed. I believe that the music he wrote for that occasion is now part of *Fanfare for the Common Man*.

BELL: Was this a multiple-network broadcast?

CORWIN: No, on one network. NBC, I believe.

But that recording was played all over the English-speaking world. It was played in Britain and Australia and all over the Commonwealth generally.

That was typical of the programs in their scope and size, though not in its theme.

BELL: That was an hour-long program?

CORWIN: No, it was a full-length concert, and I think it ran closer to two hours, topped off by the chorale of Beethoven's *Ninth*.

I did five or six big programs for the UN. *Document A/777* was an all-star affair done out here in Hollywood. That was the first big UN show that I did piecemeal and assembled from tape. The stars on it, a very impressive battery, didn't have to be there all at once as they were for my American *Bill of Rights Show*.

BELL: Can you compare those two shows?

CORWIN: I think both of them had a great deal of passion, and I think that *A/777* was a more mature program. I was more mature. Those had been a very densely packed four years of production and travel and experience and were accompanied, I like to think, by a considerable growth.

It was one of the best things I did, *A/777*. I give high marks to the structure — a roll call of the United Nations, from which I departed to illustrate instances in the history of the particular nations called, instances that inclined or obliged them to support and endorse various articles.

BELL: Were you your own engineer?

CORWIN: I was very close to being. I hovered over the editing equipment, being prevented only by union regulations from being my own engineer.

BELL: You never directed network television.

CORWIN: Not network, but television for syndication.

BELL: You never directed a live television broadcast.

CORWIN: No. *Live* television is instantaneous editing and cutting and dissolving — and so long as one grows up with that, I assume it comes easily. I've always felt lucky that in my medium, all available rehearsal time could be expended on essences rather than on angles.

BELL: Did you ever have any problems with the technical people in radio?

CORWIN: Oh, no. Whenever I put to them a problem that required some innovation, they did not come up with an automatic, "No, it can't be done." On the contrary, they were pleased to have their imaginations taxed, and they looked upon this as a welcome challenge.

BELL: Do you remember any occasions specifically?

CORWIN: Yes, when I did a program for the United Nations called *Could Be.* I wanted to get the effect of someone addressing a very large force of international volunteers assembled to do constructive work in countries that needed help. A force spread out for miles.

BELL: A Peace Corps.

CORWIN: Yes, but I deliberately used the terms of war. This army would attack, not another nation or a people, but their problems. And at dawn this force would move into action. It's all spelled out in the script, which is published in a book called *Overkill and Megalove.*
Anyway, I had a situation where the leader of this big international project stands on the summit of a hill and addresses the force below him. A reporter describes the scene:
"I am speaking from the summit of a high hill, looking down on a land that is older than the Bible" — this taking

place in the Tigris-Euphrates area. "The light of approaching day has begun to suffuse the sky to the east. In about a minute's time, the sun will edge over the rim of this bleak and desolate terrain. Below us, in a two-mile wide pass through which courses the Euphrates, is massed an army. You can't see it yet in the darkness. The first army in history to invade a country with instruments of life, not weapons of death. To construct, not destroy. On this hill is the coordinator of Task Force One, whose rank corresponds to that of a generalissimo."

Now he tells the audience what they are going to hear. "As soon as light breaks, trumpets will announce the order of the day, which the coordinator will give to amplifying trucks along the valley. I imagine you will be able to hear echoes of his voice from the sound trucks ranged at various distances along the valley.

"There it is, the first glint of the sun, the sun is rising!" And very distantly from the valley below, you hear the sound of bugles. When the last reverberations of that have faded, we hear the voice of the coordinator, who says: "Men and women, you go off to restore the earth, to heal the sick, to liberate man from hunger, poverty, and fear of age — to instill in untried peoples the confidence to do superb things for themselves. Do your jobs well, knowing that the hard-won dreams of the world rest with you."

He spoke this slowly, phrase by phrase, and I allowed time for the echo to come back at retreating perspectives. Now that was a problem that had not been handled in radio before. I had put it to the engineers, and they came up with a simple and beautifully ingenious device. Today, of course, it would just be done by patching a cord into a resonance phaser or something, but we didn't have that. We had an echo chamber, yes, but nothing that would give us a series of delays.

The device we used was a simple steel bar on which there were sliding mechanisms, something like the margin or the tab settings on a typewriter. It had a magnetic head pickup where each tab would be. By sliding the tape along these heads, you could get whatever interval you wanted by adjusting the tabs. Each head also had an individual filtering mechanism to adjust each to a different degree of filter, to give it not only delay but distance. It became a very dimensional effect. I can't tell you, really, how grateful I was and how impressed the audience was. I got letters about that, how that effect absolutely convinced them and brought them to the scene. A little device, purely technical.

BELL: Could you tell a taped show when you heard one?

CORWIN: Not really. At first, like anything new, it was a little bit unsettling. At its worst it lacked the kind of excitement and spontaneity that you get from a live, untaped performance. But on the other hand — for a man so addicted to revision as I and so upset by glitches and flaws — this was a great boon. It enabled me to correct and to make more than one take. I always envied the film director who could say, "All right, let's do it again!" Or "Take forty-six — print." We didn't have that option. Tape began to equalize that a little bit.

BELL: How many of the United Nations shows were on tape?

CORWIN: Most of them were live, but one of the biggest, *Document A/777*, was taped. *Could Be* was live, although there were taped elements within it.

Another thing about *Could Be* was that within the body of the program itself, I attacked my own concept through a speaker supposedly addressing a meeting of the United Nations. This speaker was the president of what I called the World Advancement Federation, a name so typical of those horrible, repressive outfits that cloak themselves in terms of betterment and liberty — such as The Liberty League and the Sons of Freedom — but who are usually fierce and fiercely reactionary people.

This guy said, "None of us wish to deny the enthusiasm and hope that has been aroused, but we are concerned lest this enthusiasm be short-lived. After the first exhilaration of this costly adventure, the world could be let down."

Another thing he said was, "It's frivolous to stage a mock war in this fashion since there is no tangible enemy to attack in the sense of a hostile army. The whole scheme smacks of sensationalism and dramatics. Nothing like it has ever been attempted."

You know, that line.

The response from another speaker was that the plan *was* sensational. "It was intended to capture the imagination of the world, and it has done that. As in wartime, peoples have set their minds on a goal, and they will accomplish things that they have never attempted in the past. Also, as in wartime, large things will be done by large numbers of people in a large effort."

BELL: Hasn't the pressure for a World Advancement Federation grown stronger, as regards world government, since you've written that?

CORWIN: I think it has in this country with the purging of an entire generation of liberals. In the words of Arthur Miller:

"The left wing of the eagle was cut off, and the bird has been flying in circles ever since."

They got rid of their China hands because they were too liberal for some people, and thus we lost our expertise in Asia. Then, disaster.

I think that the Liberty Leaguers have been emboldened by the attainment of the highest office. There has been nothing but success after success for those factions in the Reagan administration up to this point.

BELL: What is the media able to do independently in the political realm without being subsumed or taking on the worst tactics of the political realm?

CORWIN: The relationship between media and politics is one that is flexible and responds to the political situation. In a time of reaction, the media tend to be drugged by, influenced by, the government's attitude. Thus, the media were highly irresponsible during the McCarthy era. They went along. The media *made* Joe McCarthy.

The media can, however, be antiseptic as well as septic. It demonstrated that again with the Edward Murrow broadcast on McCarthy and with the Army hearings which ultimately brought McCarthy down.

Also, of very recent vintage, Bill Moyers's program on the secret government, broadcast last week — that being early in November, 1987 — was a remarkably frank and powerful broadcast in which the media excoriated the use of the lie in American government, particularly in foreign policy.

BELL: In *On a Note of Triumph* and *Untitled*, you make a case against those men, "back home — *publishing*." It might seem to most people that "fascism" is hardly an issue to guard against these days.

CORWIN: Fascism is a term that should be sparingly used. An editor who is opposed to a national policy, or was opposed to FDR, would not necessarily fit my definition of "fascist."

It's a right of the press to differ from popular or accepted policy. My use of the word applies to those manifestations of savage repression and tyranny that we've had from Hitler and Mussolini and Idi Amin and Syngman Rhee and Duvalier and Pinochet. That's truly fascist.

We have men in our government who think along those lines. I think that Jesse Helms is a fascist, even in his choice of idols, Pinochet one of them, I believe. He has nothing but kind words, or at least a soft approach, for South Africa which is a good example of outrageous fascism.

Last night I saw Attenborough's film *Cry Freedom* which is based on authentic material. That's fascism, apartheid is. And if any element of the media is soft on *that* —

It has nothing to do with didacticism. I don't believe in the necessity for what is too often and too loosely termed "balanced judgement" or "balanced programming." There is, I think, no other side to a lie that translates itself into wholesale murder, into war, into destruction. There is no other side to the Tonkin Bay Resolution. There is no other side to lying about the U2 flights, no other side to the lies about Iran and the Contras.

BELL: The time that you were working in radio was probably the PR height of organized labor in America, and the war years saw a great outpouring of media attention to the contributions of labor. These past forty years, according to most historians, have seen a precipitous decline of the influence of labor and exactly what "organized labor" means anymore. There seems to be a more accepted view that labor must take its piece of the blame for the decline of American economic power.

CORWIN: That's a lot of bushwah. Labor has had practically nothing to do with the decline of America's economic position. What has had to do with it is a crapshoot called the stock market, and labor is not responsible for a five hundred point plunge in one day. Labor is not responsible for hostile takeovers. Labor is not responsible for the iniquities of Wall Street — the indictable, criminal iniquities now being processed in the courts.

There have been abuses of labor, and I do not overlook them. Labor is not without sin, but its sins are relatively minor compared to the way in which it has been sinned against. I think that the deliberate erosion of labor, through the opportunism of corporate entities in the climate produced by eight years of Reagan, had a very destructive effect. Now we have rich and powerful corporations trying to get labor not only to stop asking for advances, for raises — but they are demanding retrenchment. That, I think, is a policy that can only lead us to domination by foreign economies. Our dollar is now under the value of the yen, and every other day it seems the dollar is shrinking.

You cannot lay that at labor's door, not in my view.

It's a philosophic question, a moral question. It's a question of the place of the family, of the place of the church. It's a question of national priorities, and it's a question of what the media are doing to help or hinder a return to the kind of idealism and positiveness that was in the air during the days of which you speak, when labor had a far more important place in the arch of American society. That arch has been eroded by the weakening of labor.

The responsibility of the media, especially the electronic media, is very, very heavy in this. Because of the drip-drip effect of irresponsible television, we have suffered a loss of attention. The attention span has shrunk. We find it in children who watch television for many more hours than they do homework. We find it in the kind of programs that are most popular — in the overemphasis on sports in which a Super Bowl game becomes almost a religious event, and where a commercial on that game costs $20,000 a second. A pretty high rate.

We find it in the acceleration of violence, vandalism, freeway shootings, terrorisms. The dignity of the individual has suffered. It all comes together, a kind of attitude that it really doesn't matter. You plant a bomb, and it kills twenty or a hundred innocent people, too bad. All these things are connected — related to a philosophy of gimmeism, of show-me, of what-have-you-done-for-me-lately and what's-new-and-how-fast-can-you-dance.

BELL: In *Overkill and Megalove* you introduce your poems with snippets from the news wires, quotes. It seems to be a style of your writing to take common aphorisms or ways of speaking and elevate them onto a huge stage or satirize them. Or, conversely, to take things of great meaning and treat them in the most offhand way, vernacularize them, pour on the specifics to bring them to earth.

Do you think that most information that you deal with as a writer is either to one side or the other — either much too common on its face or much too inflated on its face?

CORWIN: No, I think information is neutral if it's the truth. Some of the attitudes to which you refer are informational — Mr. Teller says that we should have army barracks and missile emplacements on the moon — and I take that and run with it. That's the information. It comes from a news story.

Mr. Gagarin, the cosmonaut, looked around and said, "I didn't see any God out there." Well, that's a statement that he made, and it's up to the writer to accept that or make a comment on it.

This is not particularly new. It's been going on since Homer. It's part of the function and obligation of a social-minded writer to exercise a capacity to comment.

BELL: It seems like those statements, that you just used, had their own center of gravity, their own agenda, and weren't exactly neutral.

CORWIN: But you see, my friend, these things *beg* for comment, yet nobody comments on them.

BELL: Can there be too much print?

CORWIN: There cannot be too much print.

BELL: Not even when it passes into trivia?

CORWIN: If you define "trivia" in terms of small and unimportant detail, the kind represented by the game *Trivial Pursuit*, there's nothing wrong or harmful in that. However, the process of "trivialization" is something else again. I addressed a whole book to that subject.

BELL: What year did you discontinue your formal position with U.N. Radio?

CORWIN: In the early 1950s.

BELL: You were with them for five years?

CORWIN: About that. I never was full-time at the UN. In my instance, I didn't want to spend my full year in New York. I had young children, and I didn't want to be away from them too long at a stretch. It was six or nine months a year at the UN.

BELL: Did you produce other writers' scripts at the UN?

CORWIN: Very seldom. They had a staff of very capable producers. There were only one or two occasions where I did so.

BELL: You were saying that you had been lucky and able to work upon invitation for most of your career, so at what point were you turning down the most work?

CORWIN: I can't spot it. I still turn down things that I don't think I'd be right for, or if the terms aren't satisfactory, but there's no line that forms outside the door in the morning. Maybe five or six times a year something comes up which I thank the tenderer for and decide not to do.
    In the active years with CBS, I was known to be a CBS man with a full agenda. Therefore, it would never occur to anybody to ask.

BELL: That's why I was thinking that this period of 1945 to 1955 might have been when you pulled in the backlog.

CORWIN: But that was also the graylist period, when the offers were fewer.

BELL: You acknowledge a graylist as well as a blacklist?

CORWIN: Of course.

BELL: What sort of an impact, in real terms, was the graylist? Were listed people underworked?

CORWIN: "Underwork" is a euphemism. The listed were denied the *opportunity* to work. "Blacklisted" — you must underscore the "black" and the "listed" both. I know people who went into sales or made a product in their garage, or went abroad in order to survive. They were completely wiped out as far as employment opportunities were concerned.

The blacklist was an iron curtain of the worst kind, impenetrable for most people. There were some who crawled and got some work that way, but the positions taken by Lillian Hellman and Arthur Miller and people of that ilk is testimony to the nefariousness of the blacklist as an expression of national morality.

In my case the economic impact was felt, but it was not grave. I wrote a book during that period, worked on some films. I did have revenue. The main impact was on my spirit. I grieved for America. I felt a betrayal of all the principles that libertarian America had evolved and defended over the years — Jefferson through Lincoln, Emerson through Whitman to Sandburg. I numbered my plays among those of a broad segment of American thought and culture, and the blacklist demonstrated how one's plays can be writ in water, can fail to reinforce even those who commissioned them — the networks. Our spirit of liberalism had been as ruthlessly suppressed as anywhere in the world, short of the kind of torture and murder that you find in the truly benighted countries.

The swing to the right that started with Joe McCarthy was pronounced, long-lasting, and devastating. The pendulum has returned a good way since then, but we are still far from the kind of position that our society occupied during the best days under FDR.

I was not alone in feeling that it is one thing for a wave of repression to hit France or Germany or Italy; but this country was fortunate in having been created by a band of courageous, idealistic, intelligent men. There are few countries that can point to their origins with the same sense of pride that we can.

For one thing, Jefferson was an infinitely better writer than most statesmen. The Declaration of Independence and other statements of American principle are of a very high order. When we skidded, we had a sharper and longer descent than countries that were older and bore the scars of previous eras of repression.

BELL: Your participation in the pair of programs entitled *Hollywood Fights Back* — made in 1948 and broadcast on ABC, paid for by the Committee for the First Amendment — was uncredited on those broadcasts.

CORWIN: I was a member of the Committee for the First Amendment which included John Huston and William Wyler and a great many of the stars, directors, and writers. I did not initiate the program but was approached by Huston or Wyler, or both, to help assemble it.

My contribution was not a terribly creative one. It was largely that of helping to produce it and guiding it to the microphone.

BELL: Didn't you write some of it?

CORWIN: I may have. What we did was to get as much as we could from the participants, to find out exactly how they felt and allow them to make their own statements. Where they felt that they might like some help in the writing of it — the rounding and polishing of what they had done — I, among others, contributed. William Robson was also a part of that. It was a striking pair of programs, very powerful, and which I hope one day will be recognized as an important document of that period. It was probably the only time that the embattled community in Hollywood *did* fight back. And apparently with some success because it made a dent in the proceedings of H.U.A.C. They suspended hearings for a time after the first program, and it was not until after the Waldorf conference that they resumed in full force.

BELL: Let me put to you the proposition that — coming out of a war in which we were in the right, back to domestic problems that were troublesome — the rich in America felt guilt at their control of so much. They still felt impelled to honor the principles Jefferson set forth, but found that communism was the only whipping boy at the time. That the only fears to attack were internal ones, and the only fear outside itself.

CORWIN: Communism has been in our century a convenient whipping boy. Just as the Jews, historically, have been convenient scapegoats; just as the Orientals, in the history of American labor, were persecuted. And of course our Indians were once prime candidates for scapegoating.

You alluded to the possibility of people of great wealth and influence feeling guilty about it. That is unlikely. Maybe now and then an eccentric individual — eccentric in the eyes of his class — may have twinges of conscience.

BELL: Let's consider those that consider themselves "liberals," then.

CORWIN: Those who truly consider themselves liberals were men like Ambassador Davies, left-thinking rich men like Thomas Lamont and the liberal industrialist of our day, Harold Willens. They are not activated by guilt. They were never activated by guilt, but by principle. Just as power is never surrendered without a struggle, neither is an *idée fixe*. And if this *idée* holds that communism is an implacable, monstrous, universal menace — then it creates all kinds of strange behavior.

Witness the daily paper. You'll find that even an event as potentially constructive and useful as Tom Brokaw's interview with Gorbachev in the fall of 1987 was immediately attacked. I'm sure that my thoughts on this subject, detailed at some length in *Trivializing America*, are not unique.

BELL: Can one still write to the United Nations and get programs that you made for them?

CORWIN: You might be able to. They are usually eager to cooperate with anyone interested in the work of the United Nations — or were, when I was on the Secretariat.

Chapter 8

BELL: Your work during the 1950s seems to have been mainly film work and stage work.

CORWIN: Yes, mainly. I wrote a couple of books in that period, too.

BELL: Norman Mailer called the 1950s the most awful decade in American history.

CORWIN: I agree. The 1950s were an awful decade. Without recourse to notes and my files and correspondence and various data that would nail down dates, I can't speak to that as readily as I can about earlier and later periods. But it was a bad period. I suffered, but certainly not nearly to the extent that many writers and directors and people in the film industry suffered. Not just the film industry — education, religion, labor — it was a miserable time, a period when reaction crested and when life for a liberal became very strained and, to some, untenable. There were suicides. There were people who were as much heroes to me as Oliver North is a hero to Reagan, dropping by the wayside, exiled, punished, jailed, ostracized. And there was the death of my medium. I had been riding a wonderful charger — a beautiful horse, the saddle and equipage of which was furnished by a great network — and that horse was shot out from under me. I suffered along with all of the other serious radio artists.

There were, of course, a lot of good people who rode right through that storm — the comedians, the Jack Bennys. But oddly enough Lucille Ball was grazed in that period because her grandfather had once signed some petition or subscribed to the *Daily Worker* or something of that kind.

BELL: How early were you approached by the movie studios?

CORWIN: As early as *They Fly Through the Air*.

BELL: Really?

CORWIN: Yes. Somebody at Warner Bros. proposed making a film of it.

BELL: You're kidding.

CORWIN: No. There is a story attached to this. When books of mine were published, I gave copies out to friends with too free a hand, and I found myself sometimes without a copy for myself. And when libraries began to collect my work, I had standing orders at a few bookshops to the effect that if this or that book of mine turned up, they would let me know.

Well, a copy of *They Fly Through the Air* did turn up, and I went down to the bookstore and got it. And inside the copy of that book was a memorandum from Ken Purdy. He wrote a good deal for *Esquire*, a fine short-story writer, and apparently at one time he worked for Warner Bros. He had written a memo proposing that *They Fly* be made into a movie, and obviously this was his copy. I wrote Purdy, telling him about my discovery. I had never met him or had contact with him. I got a lovely letter back from him.

Then, *My Client Curley* was bought by Columbia Pictures, and it was made into a bad movie.

BELL: A *bad* movie?

CORWIN: Yes, called *Once Upon a Time*. You begin with a bad title, and you make a bad movie. It was produced by Sidney Buchman, and it starred Cary Grant.

BELL: Well, that's good.

CORWIN: It didn't help the picture.

BELL: They didn't ask you to write it?

CORWIN: No.

BELL: So you really didn't have any contact with the director, Alexander Hall?

CORWIN: None whatever.

BELL: What can you tell me about Sidney Buchman?

CORWIN: He was one of the better producers, a man of great social conscience, great enough to get him in trouble with the hounds. I felt that Sidney did as well as he could under the baleful eye of Harry Cohn at Columbia. Perhaps none of the people there understood the nature of the script that they bought from me and Lucy Fletcher.

Fantasy is special material. There are not many people who are comfortable with it. Stop me before I dilate on fantasy because I have some very strong feelings about it.

BELL: The 1940s seem to have been a great time for strict fantasy films of that type in Hollywood. Do you think that might have had something to do with radio's exploitation of that story type?

CORWIN: It depends on the kind of fantasy you're talking about. If you're talking about *Alice in Wonderland*, that's already in a delicate area. We have seen many times how very few can cope with it. There have been some colossally poor films based upon *Alice in Wonderland*. On the other hand, since that time the Spielbergs and Lucases of the world have come along with big orders of fantasy. Space certainly has contributed to it, but that's *heavy* fantasy. That's blowing up planets and zooming into intergalactic battles. But when you deal with delicate matters, you are in treacherous territory.

Let me say this about *Once Upon a Time*. That picture opened in the Radio City Music Hall, and I believe it had the shortest run of any picture ever to play that house.

I met Grant at a dinner party at Richard Brooks's one night about a year later. He did everything charmingly. He charmingly and sheepishly apologized for that picture. It violated every instinct that I had about my own script. Instead of being a nebbish agent, as in my original, Cary played a producer whom we meet in black tie. This completely torpedoes the original premise.

In the original the fortunes of the agent enlarge immeasurably when he takes on the kid and his caterpillar as clients. Had I known what Meltzer was up to, I would have squawked — not that it would have done me any good because it was the studio's option. That was one of the problems of the writer in Hollywood in that day. Even in a recent yesterday, I would have had an understanding at the start that they hew to the basic concept, or I wouldn't sell them the property.

BELL: Cary Grant could play a nebbish if he wanted to. He had played them before.

CORWIN: I was told that Grant was responsible for the notion of the producer because he wanted to — and I'm using this in quotes — "dress for the part."

Also the kid, whose name I think was Donaldson, was miscast. He was a whining kid, completely unlike the boy I conceived for *My Client Curley*, who was charming. Meltzer and company had to bring in a love interest. What that had to do with *My Client Curley* I'm still trying to figure out.

It was just not right for that team. Nothing was right for it.

BELL: What did you think of films at the time like *Here Comes Mr. Jordan* or *I Married a Witch*?

CORWIN: Those were pretty good, but wherever fantasy involves realistic materials — as with *My Client Curley* or *The Odyssey of Runyon Jones* — the secret is to be logical and to play it straight. Thus, in *My Client Curley* all of the developments within the suspension of disbelief about the caterpillar itself were straightforward and logical. Musicians would be interested in why this insect of the order *Lepidoptera* would have reflexes that responded only to one tune. Scientists would certainly be interested. These developments would be quite logical.

BELL: What does having a logical narrative line in a fantasy allow you? What's the tradeoff as opposed to an *Alice in Wonderland* narrative which has a tangential relationship to logic?

CORWIN: *Alice in Wonderland* has a lot of logic, I think. After all, it's the product of a logician, a mathematician, a man whose head was in very abstruse elements of calculus and trigonometry. It's a kind of distorted logic. Alice becomes a whole series of metaphors. There are Cheshire Cats in society, and there are Red Queens in society, in civilizations that we are familiar with.

BELL: It astounds me that *They Fly Through the Air* was considered by a film studio as a property.
    I suppose it was still before our entry into the war, so its politics might have been acceptable on a certain slant, but it seems very radio-specific.

CORWIN: Well, so was *Sorry, Wrong Number*, but it made a movie. Being radio-specific does not necessarily foreclose the possibility of adaptation to film.

BELL: But it would have been an extremely condensed movie, temporally, unless they had expanded it into the parallel stories of the squadron and the village and ending with the bombing.

CORWIN: No, I don't think so. I think it could have been just as clear a statement of an attitude as, let's say, the current picture *Cry Freedom* is. And the thrust of *They Fly Through the Air* is outrage against civilian bombing which was not yet on the agenda of all warmakers.

BELL: But if you would have made a movie out of it — an hour-and-a-half film — it would have been done in real time, wouldn't it?

CORWIN: It's sheer speculation as to what the approach could have been. I think a gifted enough writer can make a melodrama out of the phone book.

BELL: What was your first film script that was produced?

CORWIN: That was *The Blue Veil* — an adaptation of *Le Voile Bleu*, a film that had been made in France. It was done for Jerry Wald and Norman Krasna when they were associated at RKO Pictures as Wald-Krasna Productions. They had had a version of it which didn't work, and they asked me if I would like to try it. I adapted it, but not all that literally. I considerably enlarged it.

It had to do with a governess, played by Jane Wyman, who took care of children and became attached to each child in turn and then had to leave that child. Along the way she meets a young man who can take her out of all this. They have a romance and are about to go off and get married when he reveals a side of his nature that frightens her off, and justly so.

She does not marry him, never marries. The children grow up, and in her later years her former wards get together and throw a party for her which is quite touching. Charles Laughton was in it. It was a picture of many episodes. I think Lee Cobb was in it, too. It won a nomination for Jane Wyman.

BELL: Tell me more about Jerry Wald.

CORWIN: Wald was co-producer with Norman Krasna. My dealings were with Krasna more than with Wald. I found that Krasna had a much better fix on the story and the whole approach than Wald. I think Wald would have liked to have been every bit as close to that picture as Zanuck liked to be close to his. But I dealt mostly with Krasna, and that was a great boon. He was a bright and knowledgeable and gifted man.

BELL: Were you on the set of *The Blue Veil* very much?

CORWIN: Yes.

BELL: Jane Wyman said that this was a role that she knew she *should* play, but that she had to be coaxed into because it was another of those difficult melodramatic roles that she did so well.

CORWIN: She was very good.

BELL: Was she a matter-of-fact worker, as even tempered as she seemed?

CORWIN: Yes, I found her to have those qualities.

BELL: Did you propose to Laughton his role?

CORWIN: I don't remember whether I proposed it to Laughton.

BELL: After the completion of that first script, you signed a contract with one of the studios?

CORWIN: No, I remained a free-lancer for quite a while. The only contract I ever signed was with Metro. Mostly I went from picture to picture.

BELL: What was the story behind Metro's lack of promotion of *Scandal at Scourie,* starring the popular team of Greer Garson and Walter Pidgeon?

CORWIN: It's my understanding that Greer and Metro had a falling out around that time, and that the studio, in an expression of impatience with her, decided it would not get behind the picture.

It's a curious thing that a studio, or any producing entity, would do that. It suggests cutting off one's nose to spite one's face. But publishers do it all the time. They bring a book out and decide that they don't want to promote it, preferring to go along on the momentum of some external buildup that might come from the subject or the author or the notices.

This is surmise on my part many years after the fact — relying only on my not-always reliable memory — but I recall that the picture opened in New York City at the Little Carnegie. That will give you some idea. The Little Carnegie was a theatre on 57th Street that, I think, seated about 300 people. So something was afoot there. That was strange.

Scandal at Scourie was, I think, an unusually good picture, perhaps one of the best that Garson and Pidgeon ever did. It was based on a true story that grew out of an incident in Ontario, Canada, having to do with the adoption, by Protestants, of a Catholic orphan who was being peddled by an orphanage that had been burned down. This was 19th-Century provincial Canada. Pidgeon was Garson's husband and the reeve of the town — a Canadian mayor.

Politically, this was a bad move for the reeve, the town being red-necked and anti-Catholic.

There had been a script written before I got on, in which the religious antagonisms had been underscored in a rather mean and painful way. Both the Catholic and Protestant expertisers to whom the studio submitted the script were appalled by it. They refused to give the studio assistance and hoped the picture wouldn't be made. But then Edwin Knopf, the producer, came to me and asked if I'd like to take a crack at it. I thought it was a charming story and made it light and pleasant without evading the problem. I handled it, I think, in a way that pulled the fangs out. I made it warm and simpatico and overcame the objections of those groups.

BELL: What were the fangs?

CORWIN: The fangs were bitterness over a nasty manifestation of religious intolerance.

I kept the basic antagonism but made strategic changes in characterization. It's a little hard to make comparisons, especially when the comparison is in my favor, between the previous treatment and my own. All I can tell you is that I enjoyed working on it. Garson told me she enjoyed the picture. But it got very little notice, very little attention.

BELL: Did you work with Jean Negulesco very closely?

CORWIN: Yes. Negulesco was a hail-fellow-well-met, a charming man, totally engaging. He had a kind of debonair, continental air. I think he was Romanian. If so, he was a good advertisement for Romania. He flattered me by saying that I had written, from a directorial point of view, a script that there was hardly anything he had to bring to. There was no reason for him to come forward with that kind of bouquet because usually directors make quite sure that they exercise their own authority, put their own stamp on a work.

I say that not in any critical sense because directors should. That's their job. But whether Negulesco profited from his fidelity to the script, or whether it damaged the film, I'm not able to say and would not venture to say.

BELL: Did you work to keep visual writing out of your film scripts, or did you feel that was part of your job?

CORWIN: I wasn't conscious of any restraint of that kind. I just wrote straight out with the tacit understanding that I was making suggestions which the director could accept or ignore. I'm happy to say that, in most cases, it worked out.

Even in some of the more important pictures, like *Lust for Life*, I was always grateful when a director would take something I had developed and bring his own creative instinct to bear on it. I took great delight in first perceiving and then acknowledging that a director had shot a better scene than the one I wrote, which sometimes happened.

BELL: You intended to write the screenplay for *All the King's Men*. When you completed it, Robert Rossen wanted to collaborate on the final draft, but you pulled out of the project.

CORWIN: That was perhaps one of my biggest mistakes. I would have had much to learn, would have greatly profited from working with Rossen. But there was, a counselor in my life at that time, now dead, for whom I had a great deal of respect and affection. He was a very important man, on the board of directors at Twentieth Century-Fox, on the board of directors of Hertz and Continental Airlines. He was a kingmaker — at one time the American business manager for Salvador Dali — all over the place. He said, "By no means will I let you do that." I listened to him when I should have listened to my better sense. He took it strictly from a public relations aspect, I suppose. His argument was that I was known as my own man — I was my own writer-director-producer. I'd never written a collaboration in my life, so to acknowledge that I needed a collaborator on this script would be to show a certain weakness. I regret that I listened to him, not because the picture turned out tò be the Academy Award winner, but because Rossen was a very good filmmaker. My work on that film was not one of my better outings to begin with.

BELL: Can you still see your script in the finished film?

CORWIN: Yes, but Rossen had the same advantage in directing his own script that I had in directing mine. In terms of the final result, it transcended the script, even his own script.

BELL: That was from a Robert Penn Warren novel of some bulk. Was that a difficult adaptation?

CORWIN: It was difficult because there were many complexities in it, many characters, a big book. I no longer have any trace of that script. I was very glad for Bob that it did what it did, succeeded as a picture, and I found it quite educational.

BELL: John Houseman came to you with the original property, *Lust for Life*?

CORWIN: Yes, it was Houseman.

BELL: Did he work with you closely on the script itself?

CORWIN: Yes, he did. It was not a matter of working with him on a daily basis, but he was of great help in the entire enterprise.

BELL: Did you two know one another from radio or theatre at that time?

CORWIN: No, we had never had a previous association.

BELL: Minnelli, then, was Houseman's directorial choice?

CORWIN: I think he was the studio's choice. He may have been Houseman's choice. I'm not clear on that. He may also have been Kirk Douglas's choice because Kirk was highly instrumental in seeing that the picture was made. He lobbied for it.

BELL: Did you work with Minnelli at all when production started?

CORWIN: Very little.

BELL: Do you remember if any great liberties were ever taken with your dialogue?

CORWIN: Yes, but that was in a picture so contemptible that I won't discuss it.

BELL: I have two credits for you that I couldn't find anything about. One was called *The Grand Design*.

CORWIN: That was a short made for the United Nations, a documentary about its work.

BELL: Did you direct it?

CORWIN: No.

BELL: *Forever and a Day?*

CORWIN: That was a war film made for British charities in which something like twelve directors and forty writers contributed. I may have been one of the contributors. Hitchcock had something to do with that, and Sir Cedric Hardwicke also.

BELL: Was that after the war?

CORWIN: During the war.

BELL: *The Naked Maja* was one of the two films directed by Henry Koster that you scripted, and one of the two films about painters that you scripted.

CORWIN: That was about Goya. I wrote it in Italy where it was produced by an Italian company. The role of Goya was played by Anthony Franciosa. Already that was enough to make me cautious. I felt he was too young, too transparently American. I took on the task hoping that, in the hands of a good director, and with smiling fortune, he could give a reasonably convincing performance.

Not only did I feel that he failed in that, but he seemed to me victim of a general self-destruct philosophy on that picture. I felt every decision made on that film was ruinous to the artistic and historical fabric.

Nothing of the kind of fidelity and authenticity that I had worked so hard to arrive at in *Lust for Life* was given the slightest welcome on that picture. It was rewritten after I left Italy, and I was so appalled when I saw a preview of it that I demanded my name be removed from it. I'm not sure if it was or not.

I must say that the director and the producers were all wonderfully pleasant people to work with, and except for injuries to art in general and Goya in particular, working in Italy was a dream.

BELL: It was the first of two pictures that you worked on with Koster, the other being *The Story of Ruth*. Who played Ruth?

CORWIN: Elana Eden, an unknown whom the producer Sam Engel found. She was an Israeli girl, and I don't think she went beyond that picture. She may have had some roles in other pictures but never had that kind of starring role again. Tom Tryon was in it, I know.

Ruth suffered from a lack of a name cast, but I have no apologies to make for that film. I think it's a good picture, and I think I did a good script. There were some people — including a very close friend of mine, a rabbi — who were appalled by the suggestion that Ruth had once been in the service of the Moabite religion. But this concept actually came from Jewish sources, particularly the *Midrash*. Historically, the film relied on whatever authoritative sources were available to us. There were no gross historical liberties taken. I did invent a good deal, but I think my invention was well within the frame of plausibility and logic.

The film got mixed notices, but it was liked in high places. Bosley Crowther hated it. I think *Time* magazine loved it.

It was a dangerous subject to take on, and the treatment was a bold one. But I have no regrets, and I think when it's compared to other biblical pictures, it does quite well.

BELL: How was the box office?

CORWIN: I don't think it made a profit, but then I don't think that *Lust for Life* made a profit in its initial release either.

BELL: Was *Ruth* a subject of your choice?

CORWIN: No. In every instance the producer came to me.

BELL: The last commercial film that I have that you have a credit for is *Madison Avenue* which was a Bruce Humberstone picture from 1963 with Dana Andrews and Eleanor Parker.

CORWIN: Yes, it was based on a book about the advertising business.

BELL: Was the book called *Madison Avenue*?

CORWIN: Yes. I don't remember who wrote the book, nor do I remember the picture, nor do I want to.

BELL: I was looking through the transcript of a seminar that you did at the Academy about seventeen years ago with Irving Stone which had followed a screening of *Lust for Life*. Is it a fairly easy task for you to paraphrase a book like

Stone's into a script, and is there a great concern for "faith-fulness" in your mind?

CORWIN: That depends completely on the basic material. If it is of a kind where it's possible to infuse imagination — to enlarge, to augment — then I would not hesitate to do so, or at least I would try to do so. However, the more substantial the basic material, the greater the obligation of the writer to be respectful of the elements that make it a singular or a great work.

Thus a popular, best-selling novel requires a different set of standards in its adaptation than the standards that would be applied, let's say, to *Moby Dick* or *Don Quixote*.

One does not lightly adapt the work of a master — in the same sense that a composer would have to wake up very early in the day and be diligent and accomplished to make an adaptation of a Beethoven symphony. I can give you an example from a recent experience.

One night I was sleepless and turned on a classical music station and heard, already in progress, a broadcast of the Beethoven violin concerto in D Minor — but it was being played on a *piano*.

I thought, "Who in hell had the arrogance, who would dare to take this great work and adapt it to piano? It was meant for the violin. Now, let's see how this brash composer, whoever he is, takes this piece and destroys it."

But he didn't destroy it at all. It was quite wonderful. It had essences and qualities that transcended even the original version for violin. I couldn't wait for the credits to be given at the end. It turned out that the composer who had adapted Beethoven's violin concerto for the piano was Beethoven himself. I had not known that there were two versions of it.

BELL: In your historical scripts, is it really possible to be faithful to history?

CORWIN: It *is* possible. I think I demonstrated that in *Lust for Life* and again in *The Rivalry* and again in *Together Tonight: Jefferson, Hamilton, and Burr*.

You depart only where you have the license to do so.

For example, *The Story of Ruth* is historic, at least it's biblical history. But there were wide-open options. The commentary on *The Story of Ruth* as it appears in the *Mishna*, which is part of the Judaic canon — even there it was speculative. Where you have a degree of speculation, you are invited to invent, to present your version.

BELL: Doesn't there come a point where the history begins to smell apocryphal?

CORWIN: Yes, there does. I'll give you an example of that. I haven't seen the movie, but I read the book. In the novel *Ragtime* there are very questionable scenes.

The author took Evelyn Nesbit and Emma Goldman, and there's a scene in which those two are together. Evelyn is lying naked in a bed, and Emma Goldman is massaging her. A young man, an interloper, is hiding in a closet and gets so excited by what he sees through a crack in the door that he begins to masturbate. He bursts out of the closet, and there's a wild scene.

Now, Nesbit and Goldman are not alive to be offended by that. I found it offensive. There is no justification, in my view, for a writer taking that kind of liberty. If it were a matter of record — if Nesbit had kept a journal or if Emma Goldman had done so — that would be another matter. There is no justification for that sort of thing when you're dealing with people who actually lived.

I wrote a piece called *Truth as a Fraction* in which I go into that whole area, and I would like you to insert it in the transcript here because this piece explicitly covers that ground.

I hope I'm not taking an antic position, nor do I think I'm being straitlaced or Victorian about this. I just have too much respect for the truth — perhaps a result of my early training as a journalist.

" . . . Historical and biographical drama does not necessarily demand unyielding fidelity to fact, nor does it impose the kind of strictures that are drawn by lawyers. The overliteral can become the underachieved in dramatic effect, and there is no excuse, not even a note from mother, for dullness. Indeed license is the birthright, if not the obligation, of every art. Without it, the mysterious afflatus we call imagination would have no place to call home. Nevertheless, dramatic and poetic license are subject to a certain decorum when in the presence of established record.

"Documentary dramatists are obliged to do right by persons and events in all matters of substance and consequence. If major fractions of truth are discounted, if there is distortion or concealment or misrepresentation or Ken Russelline self-indulgence, what comes out is a nonstatutory form of perjury. Swift, back in 1726, had Lemuel Gulliver complain that he was 'chiefly disgusted with modern history. For having strictly examined all the persons of greatest name for a hundred years past, I found how the world had been misled by prostitute writers.' Had TV and films existed on Glubbdubdrib, Gulliver might have added directors and producers . . . .

"The sacrifice of truth for what is loosely called entertainment becomes, at times, like sacrificing a child to satisfy some hungry god. There is usually wonder and drama and power enough in the whole truth without having to garnish the spread . . . .

"'Nothing is poetical if plain daylight is not poetical,' wrote Chesterton, 'and no monster should amaze us if the normal man does not amaze.' Right, G. K. Neither truth, nor pills, nor lilies need to be gilded. 'Wasteful and ridiculous excess' is what our man in Stratford called it."

BELL: In *Ragtime*, most things were so broadly stated that you were encouraged to say, "Well, they're real names, but they're only symbols now."

CORWIN: If there is an area of possibility that can accommodate such invention, well and good. But the element of taste does enter.

To have Henry Ford and J. P. Morgan meet is one thing; and for them to discuss the pyramids or the electric light or perpetual motion, that's within the realm of possibility. But I don't want to be told that Henry Ford fucked a camel.

I think that's out of bounds.

Rose and Samuel Corwin,
parents, c. 1920.

Brothers: Emil, Norman, Alfred, sitting beneath an oil painting
by their mother, c. 1913.

Norman, one year short of graduating from high school, with brothers Emil and Alfred.

Katherine Locke, actress of stage and screen, at the time of her marriage to Corwin in 1947.

Son Tony and daughter Diane,
c. 1972.

Sister Beulah, brother Alfred, with
Alfred's daughters, Vanessa and
Consuela, c. 1955.

The Corwins' first home in California, on a hilltop overlooking the San
Fernando Valley.

Walking in the country with Nick, the English setter who inspired *The Odyssey of Runyon Jones*.

Directing Larry Robinson in the original production of *Runyon Jones*, 1941.

Signalling a "sock cue" to an orchestra conductor during one of the *26 by Corwin* programs, 1941.

With Fred Allen on *Allen's Alley*.

CBS control room during a rehearsal of a broadcast in the *One World Flight* series, 1947.

For his adaptation of Edgar Lee Masters' classic *Spoon River Anthology*, Corwin assembled an outstanding cast and invited the poet to attend the broadcast. In this photo, taken following the program, are, front row (l to r): Charme Allen, Jean Colbert, Edgar Lee Masters, unidentified boy, Rosalind Gould, Ed Latimer, Luis Van Rooten, Arnold Moss; second row, Cliff Carpenter, Ann Bolen (?), Gladys Thornton, Irene Winston, Roger DeKoven, Lou Krugman, Stella Moss, Everett Sloane; at the rear, Santa Ortega, Dwight Weist.

Rehearsal of one of the *26 by Corwin* programs. Corwin at rear, with raised hand. Actor with back to camera is House Jameson; facing him, front row, Sam Raskyn, Minerva Pious, Arnold Moss, Dane Clark.

Cast of Corwin's *We Hold These Truths*, commemorating the 150th anniversary of the ratification of the Bill of Rights, December 15, 1941. It was the first four-network broadcast in radio history. Left to right: Orson Welles, Rudy Vallee, production assistant Sterling Tracy, composer-conductor Bernard Herrmann, Edward G. Robinson, Bob Burns, Jimmy Stewart, Corwin, Walter Brennan, Edward Arnold; seated, Lionel Barrymore, Marjorie Main, Walter Huston.

Stars lined up at paired microphones for the "Roosevelt Special" segment of Corwin's four-network Election Eve broadcast closing the presidential campaign of 1944. Identifiable in the line at left: Tallulah Bankhead, Irving Berlin, Virginia Bruce, Claudette Colbert, Linda Darnell, Walter Huston (partly obscured), Groucho Marx, Jane Wyman. Right line, Joan Bennett, Harry Carey, Joseph Cotten (obscured), Rita Hayworth, Rex Ingram, Danny Kaye, Paul Muni.

With Bernard Herrmann, who scored many of Corwin's productions, including *We Hold These Truths* and *On a Note of Triumph*.

Unlikely chorus in a Beverly Hills living room, c. 1959. Standing (l to r): Nunnally Johnson, Ira Gershwin, Robert Benchley, Marc Connelly, Groucho Marx, Danny Kaye; seated, Corwin and Abe Burrows.

With Gregory Peck and Peter Lorre, in an ABC network broadcast
of the Committee for the First Amendment, at the time of the
Hollywood HUAC hearings.

Claire
Trevor,
absorbed
in
Corwin's
first
published
collection
of plays,
1942.

Speaking at a dinner in Corwin's honor in Beverly Hills, in June, 1946, on the eve of his departure on the Wendell Willkie One World Flight Award trip around the world: l to r, Ona Masson, Edward G. Robinson, Paul Robeson, Robert Young, Charles Laughton.

At a military airport near Cairo, Egypt, with Col. Sandy McNown and George Polk, CBS journalist who less than a year later was assassinated by a political faction in Greece.

Interviewing inhabitants of Lanuvio, a small town in Italy hard hit by aerial bombing.

Interviewing President Eduard Beneš of Czechoslovakia, in the Presidential Palace in Prague.

In the Moscow apartment of composer Aram Khatchaturian: (l to r) Mrs. Khatchaturian, Corwin, an interpreter, musicologist Gregory Schneerson, Khatchaturian.

Press conference at La Guardia airport, New York, on completion of his *One World Flight*.

Charles Laughton, Elsa Lanchester, Corwin and Charles Vanda, production chief at KNX, having a good time with some last-minute changes in the comedy *L'Affaire Gumpert*, starring the Laughtons.

Directing sound effects for one of the *Columbia Presents Corwin* programs.

Orson Welles, cigar, and script.

With Dore Schary, head of production at MGM, and Eleanor Roosevelt, at United Nations headquarters, Lake Success.

Chatting with David Ben-Gurion, Prime Minister of Israel, after interviewing him on television, 1967. David Wolper listens in.

Corwin and Frank Sinatra, after receiving Newspaper Guild Awards, Madison Square Garden, 1945.

Jimmy Stewart, then a corporal in the Air Force (later elevated to Brigadier General) takes a snack during a rehearsal lull, 1941.

With Ken Burns, documentarian, for whom Corwin appeared on camera to open and close the film *Empire of the Air*, 1991.

Directing an adaptation of Ray Bradbury's story *The Conflagration up at the Place*, with the author at his side, 1969.

Norman Lear, Charles Kuralt and Ray Bradbury help celebrate Corwin's 75th birthday at a banquet tendered by the University of Southern California, 1985.

Going over a speech by James Earl Jones in *Bill of Rights: 200*, Corwin's extension of the 1941 broadcast celebrating the first ten amendments to the U.S. Constitution. It was carried over stations of the APR nd NPR networks.

Fifty-five years after producing his first play, *The Plot to Overthrow Christmas*, Corwin directed a revival commemorating the acquisition by the Thousand Oaks Library of his papers. The program was broadcast live over KNX from the library's auditorium. Left to right: Corwin, Parley Baer (partially obscured), Norman Lloyd, William Windom (mostly obscured), Marvin Kaplan, Samantha Eggar, David Warner, Katherine Freeman, Richard Crenna (mostly hidden by microphone), Stan Freberg, Elliott Reid, Sean McClory, Charles Champlin.

Chapter 9

BELL: You were the writer-director of a stage play called *The Hyphen*. When was that?

CORWIN: Oh, that came relatively late. There were earlier plays than that — *The Rivalry* and *The World of Carl Sandburg* and *Together Tonight*.

The Hyphen was commissioned by the University of Utah for the dedication of its on-campus theatre — a marvelous theatre that could hold its own or perhaps is superior to many of the legitimate theatres on Broadway. I wrote *The Hyphen* and directed it, and William Shatner was the star. He had already made the first episode of *Star Trek*, if that will help to date it. *The Hyphen* played in Salt Lake City for a month, the stipulated time, during which Dore Schary took an option on it for a Broadway play. He never got it off the ground.

My tendency has been not to go back and reuse previous works of mine. I get somewhat impatient with that. So I never followed through on *The Hyphen* post-Utah, though I must say there were other incarnations of the play in shorter form. One of them was done for my *Westinghouse Group W* series.

BELL: So was it a light or heavy-hearted comedy?

CORWIN: It was a comedy with a serious substratum. But you can say that about nearly every comedy of mine.

BELL: Are *The Rivalry* and *Together Tonight* both in print?

CORWIN: *The Rivalry* is. It was published by Dramatists Play Service in an actor's edition. *The Hyphen* is not.

Together Tonight is a play written around the time of the Bicentennial. Its full title is *Together Tonight: Jefferson, Hamilton, and Burr.*

The premise of the play was that the Open View Society of Philadelphia invited these three men to debate. Adams was then President; Jefferson was Vice-President; Hamilton had been Secretary of the Treasury up until a little while before; and Burr was not yet Vice-President. The irony here, of course, was that Hamilton was later to be killed by Burr.

It was a town-hall situation. There was very little suspension of disbelief, except that the men never did actually hold that meeting. It was in a theatre in Philadelphia on a rainy night.

You've heard me do negatives on myself and know that I'm not predisposed to give myself high marks for most of the things I've done. But I'm pretty good at extracting essences from texts like those of Wolfe and from the sayings and writings of Hamilton, Jefferson, and Burr.

I put the last three together in such a way — things that they actually did say — that they generate considerable passion on that stage to the point where Hamilton gets annoyed and walks off, at which point the moderator declares this would be as good a time as any to have an intermission. After the intermission there's some question as to whether Hamilton can be persuaded to come back — he's been so deeply offended.

It was no great stretch of dramatic license for Hamilton to be offended because the moderator had introduced a pamphlet that Hamilton had actually written, explaining his illicit love affair with a woman of low repute. Hamilton had published the pamphlet himself, including letters from the woman, in order to protect himself from the insinuations of his political opponents that he had used Treasury funds to pay her off.

You can see how much heat that would engender in such a situation.

The play toured the country but was not presented in New York or Los Angeles. Again, it's one of those things that I should have followed up on. It's viable. It could be produced on the boards or made into a TV special at any time.

BELL: Was this commissioned?

CORWIN: Yes. It was commissioned in its original form by Filmation, not as a project for them, but as something they wanted to back.

BELL: Was it a college theatre production?

CORWIN: Yes. It played in commercial situations as well. I think it opened on the campus of the University of Indiana at Bloomington.

BELL: They have a nice theatre there.

CORWIN: It's a beautiful theatre. Big, too.

BELL: So, the Sandburg piece falls somewhere before all these things we're talking about.

CORWIN: Yes, I can give you a date on Sandburg. It opened on October 12, 1959.

BELL: I remember seeing *The Court Martial of the Tiger of Malaya* — the TV movie you wrote.

CORWIN: That was on ABC, directed and produced by Stanley Kramer.

BELL: Tell me your impressions of him. Your work seems kindred.

CORWIN: I have nothing but the highest esteem for Stanley Kramer, both for his lifetime achievements and in terms of a working partner. I found him a superlative director.

BELL: Who had the original concept for the *Court Martial* script?

CORWIN: The subject was not my suggestion. It was Kramer's. I got the transcript of the actual trial of General Yamashita. It was another tremendous task of adaptation. The trial ran to something like 6,000 pages of transcript, going over a period of months.

The Rivalry, which was about the Lincoln-Douglas debates, was also one of those jobs of very hard quarrying.

BELL: Tell me about the research on that project.

CORWIN: The transcript of those debates — the first great one-to-one political confrontation in American history — was recorded through shorthand, in those days called "stenographic reporting." For the first time in the annals of reporting on the national scene, a debate — with all of the interruptions and catcalls and cheers and laughter and applause — was there on paper.

There were seven debates, and the total text ran to twenty-one hours with each debate being three hours long. You can imagine sifting through that and getting an extract which, in theatre time, with the domestic scenes between Lincoln and Mrs. Douglas, came down to forty or forty-five minutes out of those twenty-one hours. There were several versions of that play. It opened in a local theatre here. I directed it in a little house on El Centro, The Circle Theatre. George Boroff was its producer.

The play was bought during its run by Paul Gregory, who came to see it one night. Paul produced an expanded version in which Lincoln was played by Massey, Martin Gabel played Douglas, and Agnes Moorehead played Mrs. Douglas. I directed that production too, and it toured the country. The script was later adapted by Hallmark for a 90-minute production on *The Hallmark Hall of Fame* with Charles Durning as Douglas. A segment of it was done on *The Ed Sullivan Show*. There have also been a lot of productions in stock theatre and elsewhere.

BELL: In writing either of those two plays, either *The Rivalry* or *Together Tonight*, is it fairly difficult, either consciously or unconsciously, not to favor a character which supports your own views — Jefferson and Lincoln?

CORWIN: No, at least not for me, because I try to be controlled by a sense of justice and decency, and it turned out that many people thought Douglas was the hero of *The Rivalry*. Not because of his position, which was knocked down very effectively by Lincoln, but his was a dramatic story.

In life they were rivals in more ways than one. Douglas was enamored of Mary Todd before she married Lincoln. The two men were brought together in curious ways even before the debates. When Lincoln was defeated in the race for the Senate, he thought he was through in politics. Slow dissolve, and they are running against each other for the presidency. When the South turned ugly in its threat to secede — and it looked as though the country was headed for war — Douglas did all he could to prevent secession. He became Lincoln's staunchest ally. At the inauguration Douglas was there at Lincoln's side and held Lincoln's stovepipe hat. At the inaugural ball Douglas danced with Mary Lincoln and led the procession with her.

During the terrible days of the mounting tension, Douglas wore himself down doing Lincoln's bidding, doing what he could to save Illinois from joining the ranks of seceding states. The strain cost him his life. He sickened and died.

So, there was a lot of sympathy for Douglas's position, and I paid honor to that. The man, by his lights, had a great deal of integrity.

BELL: Do you let your sympathy for an historical figure inflect your drama?

CORWIN: I think I've been guilty of that at times. Perhaps in my earliest work, but later, no.

For example, in *Together Tonight* my sympathies and loyalties were always with Jefferson, and I had small tolerance for Hamilton, but not after I got into working on it. I felt that there were elements of Hamilton that were quite admirable.

BELL: Is the matter of threes so important to drama, as classicists might have it?

CORWIN: I suppose it does make sense. Certainly two is a requisite number. Cervantes found that out when he sent Don Quixote out on his own and realized it was not working. He brought him back to La Mancha and equipped him with Sancho Panza — gave him a foil — so that two became, not just twice one, but a thousand times more effective.

BELL: Two seems suited for the picaresque adventure, the road story, but three is something that has an axis.
  It's not uncommon in your work to find ones, acting as an axis for a constellation of connections, but not many twos.

CORWIN: That's true, I think, yes. Of course, *Together Tonight* actually was a four because I had a moderator who took an active part. The Broadway version of *The Rivalry*, by the way, had more than three characters. Five, in fact.

BELL: Rudolf Arnheim was an Austrian writer and critic who wrote an important book about film and a comparable one about radio.
  He asserts that "In art there is a general law of economy which demands that nothing but what is essential for its form be admitted in a work of art." He also wrote that there is also an economy of *enjoyment*, "that the listener is in no way entitled to supplement the work on his own, thus taking away from the representation its essential limitations."

CORWIN: I think there is a lot wrong with that.

In the first place, I am suspicious of sweeping doctrines and principles using the imperative "must." I acknowledge no such limitations, no such boundaries.

Radio, more than any visual medium, requires the collaboration of its audience. Since that is a blind audience, it must furnish its own wardrobe, decor, the physical properties of the actors, and of the entire work. If it is a worthy work, it is perceived in the imagination if it is perceived at all.

I think it is impoverishing to suggest that the audience shall enjoy no more than what it is permitted to enjoy within strictures.

BELL: He goes on to state that it is a mental jolt to conceive of an aural world as being complete in itself.

CORWIN: What claptrap! What are the visual aspects of Beethoven's *Third Symphony*?

BELL: I believe he excludes music and is thinking about drama.

CORWIN: Oh, well. That is a wise exclusion.

A passage from Shakespeare or the funeral oration of Pericles or a letter written by Vanzetti — any and all of those transcend the simple physical experience of listening. Each carries resonances that are beyond normal bounds.

BELL: Would you consider that those are conceivable theatricalizations, that the things you cite are attempts to be theatrical in themselves?

CORWIN: In response to that, I'd like to quote from an estimable critic, Kenneth Tynan.

In reviewing *The Rivalry* for *The New Yorker* he wrote, and I quote:

"By conventional Broadway standards, Norman Corwin's *The Rivalry* is not a play at all. Yet, it is unquestionably theatre. To see it is to realize with a shock of disquiet how many theatrical weapons our authors have lately allowed to rust. A stage is a platform that can serve a multitude of purposes, most of which we neglect or ignore."

Now, to the multitudinous purposes that can be served in the theatre can be added another multitude for radio or any other medium. I think that language itself, ideation, thought, expression, articulation, poetry, and metaphor can be powerful. In a truly civilized and cultured society, there cannot be conditions artificially imposed which limit the span of the audience, which decree that a speech running longer than one minute is unthinkable, which decree that a screenplay or any dramatic expression must fit into a slot. And Mr. Arnheim is, if I understand you correctly, issuing that kind of decree.

There are no inexorable laws in art. The laws are made to be broken, creatively. And when there is an unvarying obedience to laws of that kind, you invite a kind of stagnation. I'm afraid that many areas of theatre today are stagnant as a result of that.

BELL: Do you accept the premise that a theatre presentation, as opposed to a radio presentation, must necessarily be much more concerned with the question of "being" — because radio hides and distances "physical being" so well — must be much more concerned with subtleties, while radio is a storytelling medium, getting from A to C?

CORWIN: Again, by the very nature of this question, you are asking about matters that relate to formula.

You speak of getting from A to C. Well, that's a formula; that's a path; that's an indication on the map — A to C. I feel that each medium has its own properties — its own mystique and distinctness — but nevertheless that all media are related.

Radio is as susceptible of enlarging the bounds and distances and modes of transportation between A and C as any medium — perhaps more so.

BELL: Could you then entertain the possibility that narrative radio calls upon the audience to take upon themselves *more* responsibility for the plot and imagery?

CORWIN: To the extent that storytelling or narration or plot *enlists* the collaboration of the audience, they are free of their restraints that the very term "law" suggests. Law is confining, although law is necessary. I'm not proposing anarchy, although a good many artists have found that a fascinating place to go, but I am impatient with the formula approach to anything.

I think that the kinds of practical advice to be found in writer's manuals, "How to Structure" and so forth — those are all very good. They are serviceable to writers — and I do not hold them in contempt, by any means — but they do not serve the kind of writer or director who burns with the wish to do something that has not been done before, something fresh, something original that will advance, even by a small measure, the aesthetics of his art.

BELL: When you were writing radio — what mundane matters were *you* worrying about most, in terms of defining a character or setting up a space for action, and how did you work through those so that you profited later?

CORWIN: I can only say that it was not a conscious process, not waking up to say, "Today I've got to be imaginative. Today I've got to go beyond any previous norm."

I looked at my canvas and decided first of all what I'd paint and then proceeded to use whatever method I felt best served it. There were no rules to go by, which was fortunate for me. I never read texts of any kind as to how to put on a broadcast. It was all instinctual. I knew there were limitations to what you could do technically, but even those were amenable to being explored. I succeeded in broadening the frame of radio but did not set out to do so deliberately. Wherever I expanded and went beyond any previously articulated technique, it was in order to arrive at a form of expression that I felt was needed to amplify, for any purpose — expositional or narrative or atmospheric — the material. So, although I never thought of them as experimental techniques, that part of my work was a means to an end, not an end in itself.

You sometimes see a technique superimposed on a piece of work, on drama, and you realize that it is an end in itself. I've seen a number of films in which this occurred. One was entered into the Academy foreign-film competition a few years ago. It came from Japan and consisted of nothing but interiors. At the outset of a scene, you saw an unpopulated room. It stayed on the screen for a good fifteen seconds before characters entered. When they left at the end of that scene, the camera again stayed on the set for another ten or fifteen seconds. At first I thought it was an editing mistake, and then I realized it was the intention of the director or the producer or the writer or all three.

That was a technique of style. I happened to think it an extraordinarily stupid concept that served no purpose, but even if it *had* served a purpose — to use this device as a device; to say, "Nobody's done this before, and see how bright I am, how experimental, how bold, how courageous" — it is to use a technique as an end in itself.

BELL: Speaking of bare sets, the set of the radio listener is quite barer than any stage. Could you see that to have been an advantage in your more expositional works?

CORWIN: An inestimable advantage. That bare proscenium is as inviting to the radio playwright or director as a bare wall is to a muralist, as a silent organ was to Bach.

BELL: If you would devote the first ten minutes of a broadcast to setting the scene — let's say you wrote ten pages of description of the setting and blocking of the scene that was to follow, painting in words — could that be a conceivable tactic for you, or is that even a plausibility?

CORWIN: I understand where your question is coming from, but in the first place the dimensions of a space or a room are not, in the hands of a good radio script, described in so many words. They are perceived by the characters and are brought out in speech, sound, in allusions. It's done obliquely.

BELL: How obliquely *can* you do that?

CORWIN: Very, and in a thousand ways.
"Don't you ever let any light into this room? Jeez, what's that smell? Where'd you get that painting?"
"The one over the fireplace?"

"Yeah, the one over the fireplace."

"Don't sit in that chair! That's a bit rickety, an antique."

That kind of thing.

Also, I cannot conceive, in a radio play, of exact appointments and decor in the room being of that importance. They *are* important in visual media, and that's why the studios pay for set designers and sets. But note that in the plays of Shakespeare, the richest drama yet contrived, there is none of that. Bring 'em on and take 'em off, *exeunt omnes*...

BELL: Function.

CORWIN: Function. And he says: "A Cave" or "A Battlefield." That's all. Let the audience figure it out. And of course there's a good deal of theatre where that is done, that same drama of indication. *Our Town* is such a play.

BELL: Back to Arnheim again.

"In radio drama, a character exists only as it is of use, in that if one's function is small, then one's existence is small. His being is much more proportional to his function in the play than in a stage drama." This must have been liberating for you with a piece as freewheeling and abstract as *On a Note of Triumph* or as profound in function as *The Long Name None Could Spell*. That shorthand quality of the medium must have come in handy. Was this perceived by critics at the time?

CORWIN: The critics, those who did not look down their noses, perceived that. Carl Van Doren, in fact, expresses something of what you say in his introduction to my book *Thirteen by Corwin*. Certainly, Archibald MacLeish and

Stephen Vincent Benét were comfortable in making use of that viewless proscenium.

BELL: Did you think, after gaining your success, of doing another poetry program?

CORWIN: No, I never felt I had *left* poetry. What was *On a Note of Triumph*, really, but a poem? I took pains in the preface of the published version to say it *wasn't*, but it nevertheless has the characteristics of a poem. So did *The Long Name None Could Spell*. So, in a sense, did *Document A/777*. So, in a sense, did parts of *Could Be*.

If you meant by that question, did I ever think about going back to the adaptation of the work of others? No, I didn't. I realized this was a phase that I went through to the satisfaction of people like those who carry on what is now called Reader's Theatre. That's now coin of the realm.

BELL: So it wasn't coin of the realm when you did your Sandburg play?

CORWIN: Well, that was long after I did *Words Without Music*.

BELL: But that concept for theatre, did you get the idea from anyone in particular?

CORWIN: No, again, the technique was in the means of saying it. *The World of Carl Sandburg* is a very good example of what I'm talking about.

The genesis of *The World of Carl Sandburg* was not some producer coming to me and saying, "Could we do an evening of Sandburg with a cast of three?" It began when I was approached by a man who said he would like to put on an evening at Royce Hall to benefit the Braille Institute. That got changed later to benefit UCLA Scholarships.

BELL: Do you remember why that change was made?

CORWIN: Oh, external problems, questions. I undertook it as a work of friendship for Sandburg. I accepted no fee for it. I put together an evening in which there were not three, but about twenty people. For the Broadway and road version, I compressed it from twenty characters to three.

BELL: Did you have to cut out any of the poems you originally used?

CORWIN: It was essentially the same substance but served a different purpose. The theory, approach, and spirit were different. One is not better than the other — they were different.

BELL: Did you have a folksinger character at Royce Hall?

CORWIN: Not as a character, but there were songs sung, of course.

BELL: By many different people?

CORWIN: Not many. One or two.

BELL: There's a sense in some of the songs that you chose, in Sandburg's general treatment of history as well as your own — something not quite disrespectful or incorrect but flippant. Putting history into the common tongue with snazzy words and irony.

CORWIN: Sure, anything can be made funny.

Take a two-liner about something very serious — death. There's a knock on the door. The voice from inside says, "Who's there?" A voice answers, "Death." The voice inside says, "Death who?"

One can take the gravest things and make them funny. That doesn't come within the purview of my earlier-stated objection to falsification and to attributing motives or acts or thoughts to someone who actually lived. If I read a biography of the Duke of Wellington, I don't want the biographer to invent liaisons or battles or motives. But there's nothing *sacred* about history. There is no sign on the door that says you can't kid the Battle of Blenheim if you can do it or that you can't poke fun at Adam and Eve.

BELL: Do you think of history as something tainted by those who have had their hands on it?

CORWIN: History is usually the story as told by victors, and it is very seldom that you get the minority report. Those minority reports sometimes take remarkable form. They become revelations; they are sensational when they come up.

Gore Vidal's biographies are good examples. He interpreted Abraham Lincoln as a victim of syphilis, and I feel that did no particular service to history or to Lincoln. I'm willing to take this version into account if he's able to substantiate what he reports. The question of whether it matters or not is another consideration.

BELL: Did you read his book on Aaron Burr?

CORWIN: Yes, I did, and I thought it a pretty good book.

BELL: There wasn't anything outrageous in it.

CORWIN: No, nothing like that. But Burr was a very colorful character, and you didn't have to invent much for him. It was all there.

BELL: Was it your idea, or was it your publisher's to print the Broadway script of *Carl Sandburg*, on the right-hand side, juxtaposed with your conversations with Sandburg?

CORWIN: That was my idea.

BELL: Where did those conversations take place?

CORWIN: At the Bel-Air Hotel. I took a tape recorder over, and I sat Carl down and asked those questions.

BELL: He was working at Fox at the time?

CORWIN: That's right.

BELL: Did he ever have any real projects for Fox?

CORWIN: No, George Stevens hired him to work on *The Greatest Story Ever Told*. It was an impractical arrangement.

BELL: As a children's author, do you think that he was a good writer for children?

CORWIN: Well, I would have to get into the mind of a child to answer that question properly. What we sometimes think is good for children turns out not to be so good for them when a jury of children delivers its verdict.

Alice in Wonderland is not a book relished by children. It's far too sophisticated. My own *Odyssey of Runyon Jones* is not for children, even though it has to do with a child. Much of *Sesame Street* is not for children. But Sandburg had a wonderful vein of nonsense, and this was not forced. He loved puns. He loved to think and talk about Hongdorshes and Hoomadooms. He was already old when he wrote those poems, but the child in him was never suppressed.

BELL: You are, in your radio books and in the Sandburg book, always very meticulous about your performance notes, both anecdotal and aesthetic. Are they suggestions only?

CORWIN: Sure, they're suggestions. You know, very often an artist finds himself on the receiving end of suggestions. The typical one is when the playwright or director has a preview, and a friend comes to see it and says, "Well, I think it needs work."

There are times when a suggestion is valuable and immediately applies. There are other times when it is, I'd even go so far as to say, obnoxious. There are times when you say, "Yeah, that could make sense." Other times you'll say to yourself, "I can forget this. It's a lot of hogwash."

It's the old story of ten directors addressing the same scene, and each directing it his own way. There are no two thumbprints alike, and there are no two directorial points of view alike. Sure, in a collaborative medium many opinions and judgments can come into play, but ultimately it comes down to the imprint of a single person with authority. When it doesn't, the results show. It becomes a mess. It's amorphous. For good or ill, there's something to be said for the *auteur*.

BELL: To link that to thoughts about media specificity again, are there media in which "amorphous" works better than in others? Better in the theatre than onscreen?

CORWIN: You must be speaking of deliberate and planned amorphousness.

BELL: Let's say it just happens.

CORWIN: Accidental amorphousness? There's nothing to be said for amorphousness. Then you are reduced to oatmeal. It's featureless, and I think that the mind of the audience wants to be led, wants to be directed, in the same way that a growing child wants to be, needs to be, directed.

BELL: Do you find anything depressing in that statement?

CORWIN: No. Nature itself seeks order. Nature in its highest manifestations is very orderly. There is a lot of chaos, but when you consider the interacting systems of gravity, the solar system, the galactic spirals; when you consider atomic structure, molecular structure, the laws of ordinary phenomena like crystallization — every grain of salt obeys structural laws and is a cube.

BELL: Isn't nature structural in being but entropic in action?

CORWIN: Certainly, I'm not saying that there aren't vast areas of amorphousness in nature. There's a great deal of violence and unpredictability and imbalance, but we could not have evolved as the marvelous engine that a human being is — the wonderful amalgamation of the senses —

without inexorable and beautiful and dynamic and powerful laws of structure being exerted.

It's as Whitman says, "A mouse is miracle enough to stagger sextillions of infidels, and the narrowest hinge in my hand puts to scorn all machinery." A machine is structure. We are structure. We are a machine.

But what splendid variation and outreach there is in the human machine.

BELL: Then of what use is planned amorphousness?

CORWIN: Planned amorphousness is something else. The very term "planned" suggests structure.

In the plays of Harold Pinter, the characters who appear on the surface to be boring and repetitious and amorphous are far from that. On the contrary, in the hands of a John Cage, for whom I have very limited and hard-arrived-at appreciation, there is often a planned amorphousness that is only silly and unproductive. It's amusing, but not to be taken seriously. Such as when a pianist comes out to play a piece called "4:33," sits at the piano for four minutes and thirty-three seconds with his hands in his lap, and then gets up and walks off. That is planned amorphousness.

BELL: It's a joke.

CORWIN: It's a joke. That's right.

BELL: Planned amorphousness is a good way to get a laugh.

CORWIN: Well, so is coming onstage with your fly unbuttoned.

Don't misunderstand me. I have respect for differing aesthetics, and I feel that my life might have taken a different turn if I had enjoyed the same kind of workshop that Eugene O'Neill and Arthur Miller enrolled in. They certainly were exposed to theory. It so happens that when I serendipitously found myself producing for a network, the demand and the scheduling and the time required to write, direct, and produce that many programs under great pressure precluded my ever taking the time off or enjoying that luxury. I have high regard for good teaching and good theory, and I do not give myself any extra ribbons for being self-made, as it were.

Chapter 10

BELL: I'd like to ask you about a few of the radio writers who were your contemporaries.

Stephen Vincent Benét did some radio work.

CORWIN: He was one of my heroes. I think he was a great poet. *John Brown's Body* is the one truly great American epic poem. He wrote a script for the series *This Is War!*, which I had something to do with.

BELL: Arthur Laurents?

CORWIN: I directed one of his scripts, and he was a good craftsman — and better than just a craftsman. He had a lot of good things to say, and he said them well.

BELL: Fletcher Markle?

CORWIN: Fletcher is one of the best of breed. He's a splendid writer, and I almost regret that he went so far, so fast as a director and producer. I feel that if he'd had more occasion to write, he would have left us with a wonderful legacy of radio scripts.

BELL: I noticed in looking over a list of correspondence that you have corresponded with quite a number of the

so-called Hollywood Ten: Alvah Bessie, John Howard
Lawson —

CORWIN: I can't recall particular items of correspondence,
though I can say that some on that list were postcards or
single items. The extended correspondence was with Van
Doren, with Benét, with Sandburg — but there are perhaps
a number of people from whom I heard only once.

BELL: Tell me more about Carl Van Doren.

CORWIN: I first met Carl Van Doren at a writers
conference at Boulder, Colorado. In my freshman year at
CBS, I had been invited to participate on the strength of
Words Without Music. You may recall my saying that when I
got on the air with that series, I became of interest to writers
and poets. The invitation to attend this writers conference
was typical. It also represented my first trip west of Chicago.
    I met Van Doren on a mountain top. I liked him very
much, and he became a fan of my broadcasts. He was a
marvelous patriarchal figure to me. Not in the sense that he
was a counselor who gave me advice, but he was a Pulitzer
Prize-winning biographer of Franklin, and he had
enormous dignity. He was a man of great eminence.
    It's a pity that a name like Van Doren slips beyond the
ken of students and scholars today. He selected my play
Daybreak to be part of an anthology called *Three Readers* for
which Clifton Fadiman, Van Wyck Brooks, and Van Doren
were the reader-editors. I found myself in that book with
Thomas Jefferson and others of pretty high mettle.

BELL: Did you ever meet Brooks?

CORWIN: Just to say hello.

BELL: Gertrude Berg, Dashiell Hammett.

CORWIN: Only one from Hammett, but I met Gertrude Berg several times.

BELL: Rex Stout, Goodman Ace, Herbert Bayard Swope.

CORWIN: Stout and I were together on the Writers War Board. Swope spoke at the *One World Flight* luncheon for me at the Waldorf. Goody Ace kept a collection of my *26 by Corwin* series which he recorded off the air.

BELL: Rod Serling.

CORWIN: We were very good friends. We didn't see each other very often, but there was mutual high regard. In a doctoral thesis written about my work, the writer Carolyne Malloy solicited from Serling, among others, comments about me. Those letters exist in an appendix to her book. There is a very touching letter from him. He was very warm in his regard for me as I was for him.

BELL: Was he a person addicted to work?

CORWIN: That I don't know. I would gather from his output that he was, but there are some workaholics who seem to take it in form. Their stride is even, and they don't seem to sweat. Ray Bradbury is one, and Serling was another.

Serling was all over the place. After all, doing the narration for the Cocteau films was no small chore. I don't think that either Ray or Rod were my kind of worrywart-workaholic — with my penchant for never being satisfied, never really feeling finished with a script.

BELL: Were you ever petitioned to write scripts for the big TV shows — *The U.S. Steel Hour, Playhouse 90, Omnibus,* and the like?

CORWIN: No, I never felt the need for that as a kind of commercial *Good Housekeeping* stamp of certification. I did big shows. They don't come any bigger than a four-network show. Those big sponsored programs you mention didn't have the lure, the pull to me, that they might have had for other writers. I think that had I expressed an interest and had I said to my agent, "Let 'em know down at Kenyon and Eckhart" — I might have been invited. But I was generally considered by the trade, as far as I could tell, to be a sort of self-contained and sustaining Joe, off doing his own thing.

BELL: There might have been a certain amount of feeling, then, that it wouldn't have been worthwhile to ask you at all.

CORWIN: That may have been the case. The terrible truth of it is, and I say this with sorrow, that I had to be *invited* to do all these things — *Lust for Life, On a Note of Triumph,* the *Bill of Rights Show.* The invitations then became commissions — these are the terms, and here's your date, and this is the budget. I sound the note of sorrow because I would like to be able to say to you that I was seized with an inspiration to do something and dropped everything, to the exclusion of everything else, and went ahead, *driven,* to do this or that. But I was not ever in that position, and that may have worked to my ultimate disadvantage. I hope not.

BELL: Why would you like to be able to say that?

CORWIN: Because I should like to do certain things out of pure curiosity or impulse — pure drive — out of the need to do it, out of the wanting keenly to do it. And instead, I was spoiled as far as my own psyche was concerned, spoiled by being invited so much. I'm *still* being invited.

I've learned to say no to the things that I don't want to do or don't think would produce much, but I wish I'd said no to a great number of things.

BELL: But it's right and proper to receive invitations if you have a reputation and a good body of work. You're talking about regrets in the past, and not the way things are going now?

CORWIN: That's right.

BELL: What are the most pernicious aspects of the artistic game?

CORWIN: There are two kinds of perniciousness — external and internal. The external includes knaves and crooks and slobs and muttonheads and venal characters who are sometimes in places of power. I don't have to name them. They are part of the history of all the media. Just as, on the other side, there are wonderful people by whom one is enriched in work or through any other association. But those are the external.

The internal perniciousness is self-doubt or, in my case, a tendency never to be really satisfied with what I have done. There is the ordering and structuring of one's time and one's life — whether one has enough balance; whether you get enough rest, take vacations, enjoy the company of friends; whether you're a party man or permit yourself to get distracted. Honoré de Balzac had a terrible weakness for bad business deals. Mark Twain suffered from the same thing. Those are internal things, a matter of character, a matter of psychological roots.

BELL: Is it difficult to maintain open-hearted admiration for the great works of people that you modelled yourself upon, without being overwhelmed, intimidated?

CORWIN: One has to be careful there. It's a far-reaching question. One can either be so intimidated by the majesty and power of a Shakespeare that you're paralyzed, or you can enjoy his genius and be inspired by it. All my life, I find that whenever I refresh myself by listening to or reading the great masters, it is important to make allowances for the limitations in one's own art. At the same time, not to be content to stay within those limitations. As Browning wrote, "Ah, but a man's reach should exceed his grasp, or what's a heaven for?" While it's one thing to say you're never going to write like Mozart or Dickens, that doesn't mean one should necessarily settle for a safe set of limitations. One should *try* without battering your head against a wall. One should court inspiration — whether through visiting great paintings in a museum or listening to music or reading great poetry; whether it is dining with Emily Dickinson or, across the room from her, Will Shakespeare.

BELL: Do you feel you were privileged to be one of those writers who seemed not to have to touch their own lives? Not that you didn't use the lessons of your life, but you had to use relatively little of the actual stuff of it.

CORWIN: Yes, that's quite true. But I ask you, how much of the personal as against the impersonal is represented in a Diego Rivera mural?

BELL: It would be easier if you would make comparisons with other writers.

CORWIN: Let me do that for you. It's quite a justified observation, what you say. There are writers like Proust, Kafka, Dickinson — to an extent Blake — who were directed inward, who constantly took their own pulse and did so with striking effect. But, as for myself, I never felt that the elements of my life — the personal, inward elements of my life — were sufficiently singular to occupy time that I might otherwise spend writing for a bigger canvas. Not that the personal cannot be very, very big. But I ask myself how much was singular about all my experiences, observations, the women in my life, the friendships in my life; how much there is to convey? It's true that every person has a novel in him, theoretically, but it's like Frank Harris's book on his sexual adventures — luridly and sometimes beautifully expressed. In that department he damn near said everything that need be said.

What I am saying is in a sense a cop-out, this rationalization of why I have not written personally. I have allowed myself every now and then to write about people. I did it in *The Blue Veil* which was mostly invented — although it was based on French material of which I used very little. And I did it in a number of other pieces, sometimes in a slight way. I think *Scandal at Scourie* has sensitive writing about people. So, I know that I can do it.

At this stage of my life, and I'm closer to seventy-eight than I am to seventy-seven, I've even been thinking of writing a novel. My publisher wants me to write a novel. I have not written one, although there's an item of misinformation in the Random House Dictionary that says I'm a dramatist and *novelist*. I should like to justify them, and I may do that. What attracts me to the novel is that it's a big challenge, and it would lay to rest for myself, as well as those interested enough to ask, the questions about why I have not written other than on an impersonal level most of the time.

BELL: Is there a compunction in yourself, in your makeup, against stealing other people for a book?

CORWIN: There is that element, yes. I must confess that it is present, as well as the consideration of stealing from myself, but I don't think it's insuperable by any means. I tend to be a private person, and I try, though I'm not always successful, not to wear my heart on my sleeve.

But there are depths and depths. I indict myself for not writing short stories or novels, for not writing enough poetry. I don't write poetry as poetry. I am appalled that I never wrote a love poem to a person. I wrote a quasi-love poem that appears in *Overkill and Megalove,* but again it's a kind of abstraction. I've written love letters — not many of them, but I'm afraid that they were more literary than human. That's too harsh a judgment, but I have all kinds of reservations about my performance and my record as a writer of inward contemplation.

BELL: Have you got an outline for the novel yet?

CORWIN: No, no. But I never have an outline before I begin. It's all chaos.

BELL: When someone refers to you as the "Shakespeare of Radio" — the past-master figure — does it sadden you that you are no longer writing for special audiences at the Old Globe? That you are ex-Radio?

CORWIN: I'm not ex-Radio. Radio is ex-America.

BELL: The final words of Irving Stone in the seminar you gave together were, "Write books. Everything else will be diluted."

CORWIN: Well, not quite true. The force of a personality, the power of an artist, if he achieves that power — and there are many men who do have that power — can overwhelm censorship.

Cry Freedom does not suffer from censorship. It is not as if the American government said, "Hey, wait a minute, we think that this is unfriendly to a country that we are not at war with." Men like Spielberg and Lucas can do pretty much as they damn please, so long as it doesn't violate normal tolerances.

BELL: Did you see *The Color Purple*?

CORWIN: I saw it. I didn't particularly like it, but I thought it a step forward for Spielberg. I was glad to see him do something besides the very high-grade schlock of his previous films.

BELL: Who are your favorite film directors?

CORWIN: Huston. Fellini. DeSica. Attenborough at his best. Buñuel.

BELL: Did you ever attempt to write a script consciously Hustonian, or as Buñuel?

CORWIN: Not as directly as that, no. There may be a general overarching influence. I remember once going to see at the Academy two features in the foreign-film competition. The first was that dreadful Japanese film that I mentioned before. I was almost sick from exhaustion, but I thought, "Maybe I'll see the first reel of the Buñuel film that follows." That film was so marvelous that I was no longer fatigued. It was as though I had had a night's rest — it refreshed me so much.

That is what great art can do. While many other instances of finding a work of art are not as dramatic and pointed as that one, the long-range influence has been there. I feel that my early intoxications with Keats — or even good journalists like Heywood Broun — became part of my germ plasm, part of my entire literary and artistic corpus.

BELL: If someone made the contention to you that our world and our necessary everyday grasp of it has become so complex in comparison to the necessary comprehensions of Shakespeare or Austen or Dickens, that non-fiction or journalism may now have more possibilities to it than the fictional novel — how would you respond?

CORWIN: I don't think that journalism will ever have more possibilities than the novel. Never, by the way, is a long, long time. But on a somewhat shorter term, I don't think it will achieve that. Not to downgrade journalism, which can be a high calling.

It's a very complicated world, and journalism not only copes with it but transcends it. The complications of the world are what makes journalism. It's complicated when the stock market plunges 500 points in a day, but it's also a great story. So is war, and so are reporters hiding in the bushes outside Mr. Hart's house. Sometimes a story is as contemptible as that.

But to a Jane Austen or a Dickinson or a Will Shakespeare, it wouldn't be easy today. Goddamn it, they'd have to go out and obtain smog certificates before they could get the registration for their cars. They'd have to pay estimated tax; and they'd constantly be besieged by people wanting handouts, constantly be asked to speak or teach courses in dramaturgy; and Emily Dickinson would be a writer-in-residence at Wellesley or something like that. It is a different world. There is no such thing as an ivory tower. There is no such thing as going off to Tahiti. The world is populated by a couple of billions more than it was then, and it's getting more crowded.

BELL: Is there something wrong with writing poetry about smog certificates?

CORWIN: Certain poets are brought up in this milieu, are able to do it and do it well. Sandburg was a colloquial poet. In a sense Masters was, and so was Kenneth Fearing.

BELL: But the colloquialism in the case of those men was used to present an affirmative and sentimental vision of mankind.

CORWIN: Yes.

BELL: Wouldn't smog certificate poems tend to be less affirmative?

CORWIN: Well, you can be nihilistic and negativistic and write good poetry.

BELL: But is there a garden path here that someone is being led down?

CORWIN: I don't think so, no. A true poet, a great artist, can paint murals lying on his back. He can write *Don Quixote* in prison, or he can be in a little shack on Walden Pond and do well.

BELL: I suppose a more cogent way of asking this question would be to ask if you feel a too-strong undercurrent of helplessness, victimization, lack of control in art today — as opposed to *Spoon River Anthology*?

CORWIN: Yes. I think that victimization puts it pretty harshly; but in the larger sense, our whole culture is victimized by trivialization, victimized by menaces that did not exist in previous eras, monopolistic practices like Gulf & Western taking over Paramount, General Motors taking over Random House, or whatever conglomerates are participating. General Electric is now the owner of NBC. This kind of thing can only have a deleterious effect that will filter down to the individual artist and hurt him. Hurt us all.

BELL: Is there a foreseeable ending, reversal, or a coming to terms?

CORWIN: I'm not a good prognosticator. I can only answer that by saying that it is not foreseeable to me, but that is not to say it is not possible.

Everything is so interrelated in this world — war and peace and prosperity and depression — that the only hope is for a point of saturation to be reached. As in Paddy Chayevsky's *Network*, we will get damn mad and have had enough of it. There have been cases where suddenly there is a tide — there is an upswell of resentment — and things change.

We've seen the sexual revolution. In a smaller compass we see the anti-smoking revolution. After a while people got fed up and said, "Wait a minute, *no* smoking on airplanes." I remember when travelling on flights you were given complimentary cigarettes as a come-on. Philip Morris would have a nice little package, three cigarettes.

BELL: Is the spectacle of General Electric absorbing NBC as disturbing to a young person today as it would have been to a young person in 1940?

CORWIN: It's a much more powerless world today than it ever was in 1940, notwithstanding that Europe was already into World War II. It's a more dangerous world because it's a more crowded world, to begin with, and the technology for destroying ourselves is much more advanced. It's a world in which, for the first time, people can't even be secure that the ground they walk on and the water that comes through their pipes is not poisoned. This didn't exist on such an enormous scale in 1940.

Moreover, the erosive effect of eight years of Reagan and the years of Nixon and the red-neck philosophy of the right wing — all of these downgrading influences have reduced the capacity of our people to act for themselves and think for themselves. Now, more than before, we are getting the landslide effect in national elections. I don't despair yet of the American capacity to regenerate, to renew the stamina and fiber of our people, but I think that we're living in an age of mediocrity and that the people who are the gatekeepers of media and communications are mediocrities. They struggle *against* quality.

There are breakthroughs; there are exceptions. Thank God for those. But they become more and more isolated.

BELL: You said once that we should take care to rewind freedom and liberty like a faithful clock. Where does this country go when the gruel is too thin and the clock runs down at once?

CORWIN: What happens is that a country goes into decline. It's not novel in the experience of the human family. We've had nations that were relatively more powerful in their world than we are in ours — Rome and Spain and Persia, for example — and they went down.

It doesn't happen overnight. But there *is* decline, and prosperity has a price. So does power and the arrogance generated by power. It is very costly — the arrogance of people like the Nazis. They are going to find out in South Africa, if they haven't already, that arrogance will cost a great deal of blood and agony, but ultimately apartheid will be destroyed.

My worry is that we are on a course of decline, notwithstanding our armaments and our per capita income and the number of telephones and automobiles we have. The raw-boned people who are not eating white flour and not giving children sugar-frosted cereals in the morning — people who lack almost all of the amenities that we take for granted — may be the power of the next century.

One could retire into the comforting thought that, as one can trace glacial epochs and retreats, civilizations will rise and fall — rise again somewhere else and then decline. But cyclical-pendulum alternations and progressions can now be interrupted or ended by just the use of a dozen or so missiles.

You begin throwing around hydrogen bombs, and you forget it. There will be no such thing as regeneration except on the most primitive terms.

BELL: We don't really need to speak of technology or economics as a reason, strictly, for decline?

CORWIN: Yes, that's true. We don't.

BELL: Then, your plays for radio, where does this glaciation place them today?

CORWIN: I think that as long as there are histories of radio or tapes on any shelves, I will have represented an epoch, a certain era, in radio. Of course there is no reason why I cannot be superseded by radio playwrights of the future.

BELL: Do you listen to much of the current BBC radio output?

CORWIN: Whatever comes through. There isn't much in the way of serious BBC material that I hear in radio. Of course, we have *Masterpiece Theatre* and all kinds of imports on public television, but the day-in day-out product of the BBC in radio does not get much circulation in this country, as far as I know. Two exceptions to that are the two Saturday evening programs on KUSC — I don't know if they are also carried by the American radio network or any of the NPR stations — but they are not typical of what the BBC is capable of doing in drama. These are simply game shows — rather superior ones — but nevertheless highbrow game shows in the way that *Information Please* was, except more versatile.

BELL: It seems that what gets bought by public radio are the gentleman detective shows, the quintessential British stuff, the nine-part *Bleak House* type of thing.

CORWIN: There is a kind of low-level of entrepreneurship in that respect. Perhaps I'm being condescending. By "low-level" I mean the revival of the kind of radio that was broadcast for the middlebrow listener — suspense shows, cops and robbers, the Hi Brown programs. I have not once been asked to release or contribute any of my material to that process. I'm talking about old programming of mine, the revival of old shows.

Now and then, I've heard of people flying across the country and listening to a tape playback of *On a Note of Triumph* on those flights where they have multiple-choice listening, but I never received any request for permission, nor, I hardly need add, have I received any royalties.

BELL: That's one particular program that was released commercially on disc a long time ago.

CORWIN: That's right, yes.

BELL: It seems as if you should receive royalties, certainly.

CORWIN: I think I need an agent to look into that.

BELL: Perhaps people don't ask you because they think you would simply refuse.

CORWIN: That's no reason not to ask because if I were hard-nosed about it, I would find out and proceed to sue or bring action against them. It's not public domain. I don't know how they assume that. I've just been too preoccupied with things to stop in my tracks and go through the necessary steps to initiate action.

BELL: You see those tapes of radio in drug stores and such. No company has come to you and said, "Let's release a series of tapes"?

CORWIN: No.

BELL: That really is surprising, unless there might be some assumption that your material was terribly topical and couldn't connect today.

CORWIN: But it wasn't. My material does stand that test, in large part. Certainly the war stuff was topical, but I can name a dozen plays right off, without thinking, that are not. *The Plot to Overthrow Christmas* is not topical. *The Undecided Molecule* is not topical. *My Client Curley* is not topical, except in minor details.

Of course, *On a Note of Triumph* and *Untitled* are topical, but why do they stand up? Why do people still play them? I assume it's because they still have interest in what the programs have to say about an era, an important event, a great milestone and a major tragedy in the history of civilization.

BELL: In the early 1950s you published your children's book, *Dog in the Sky*.

CORWIN: It was based upon the original broadcast of *The Odyssey of Runyon Jones*, but considerably embellished, vastly embellished.

BELL: Was that an easy one?

CORWIN: It was a romp, and I greatly enjoyed it. It subsequently had various incarnations.

Ray Evans and Jay Livingston — the writers of "Que Sera Sera" and other outstanding movie music — came across this book and called me and said that they wanted to make a musical based on it, as Rogers had done with *Samson*. I agreed and helped them, and they wrote a spanking score. It was staged under my direction in a theatre-in-the-round bigger than Grand Central Station, out in Woodland Hills, way the hell out on Ventura Boulevard. The theatre has about two thousand seats, which was of course a terrible choice.

It was produced by the late Nick Mayo, a first-class fellow. It enjoyed a fine cast and was quite a bright work. Mayo made the unfortunate decision to open it around Christmas time, a notoriously bad season for theatre box office. The work was respectfully reviewed, but it lasted only about two weeks or so.

Later on there was a version called *Odyssey in Progress* which was done on my *Westinghouse Group W* series in Toronto. In it I played the part of Father Time, behind a flowing beard and makeup.

The musical is still a viable work. Maybe someday, after I'm gone, somebody will discover it. Later, the material attracted NBC — a good seven or eight years after the Woodland Hills production. NBC spent a lot of money to buy the rights, and I prepared a draft for them. The producer for whom I prepared it was displaced in a palace revolution, and a new producer inherited it who was as wrong for this piece as I would be wrong for running NASA. This producer set to work within an extremely limited concept of what the material called for, then reassigned it to a sensationally untalented rewriter, and the whole thing was trashed.

BELL: What year was this?

CORWIN: Maybe four or five years ago. That was the end of that. It was going to be a 3-hour TV movie.

The Odyssey of Runyon Jones was a favorite story of James Thurber, by the way. It was Thurber who suggested that I make a novella of it. He suggested it to Jack Goodman of Simon and Schuster, my publisher, who relayed it to me. On Thurber's say-so alone I went ahead.

Chapter 11

BELL: Was *Between Americans* the first telecast of one of your plays?

CORWIN: No. It was *Untitled*, when CBS was still housed in Grand Central Station. That was produced by Gilbert Seldes, and I think Worthington Miner had something to do with it. It was very favorably reviewed by *Variety*.

BELL: The late 1950s through the late 1960s seems to be a period when you were producing few books, fewer scripts, and that you didn't have an ongoing production schedule with anyone that I know of.

CORWIN: For eight years I wrote a monthly column for *Westways* called "Corwin on Media." That was in the '70s and into the '80s, from 1973 to 1980.

BELL: That was during that same period that you were writing *The Rivalry* and *Together Tonight*.

CORWIN: And *Cervantes*.

BELL: That still leaves us with the period of ten years before that. *The World of Carl Sandburg* was published in

1961, and *Overkill and Megalove* was published in 1963. So, from 1963 to 1973, what was happening?

CORWIN: I did some teaching at UCLA during that time. I taught drama writing. I was also a writer-in-residence at the University of North Carolina during that period, and later at Santa Barbara. I had lectured at Indiana University then, too.

BELL: Did you fall into academia then, by invitation?

CORWIN: It began by invitation. I did fall into it. It was never an ambition of mine, and I at first doubted whether I could fit into the picture because I had no formal education beyond high school.

BELL: The first work you did was at UCLA?

CORWIN: Yes, but both during and after the radio years, I was invited to speak occasionally at Rutgers and Harvard and various southern California colleges. I taught during those interim years. I was on the faculty of the School of Fine Arts of the University of Alberta in Banff. I hopscotched around, typical of the pattern I described earlier, where these invitations would arrive, and I'd accept whatever appealed to me.

The other day I got a call for still another such thing. I'll weigh it and see if I want to do it. This isn't to say that I'm invited to all the dances. I speak of it in a tone of complaint because I wish to hell that I would determine to do things without recourse to invitations. Turn 'em all down and attempt something of size and scope.

The things that I really would like to do I have the feeling wouldn't get off the ground commercially. I'd like to write an epic poem of the weight of *John Brown's Body*. I will never do it, though.

BELL: Can't you arrange something with the USC trustees, giving you sabbatical until you finish the poem?

CORWIN: I can afford to take the time now, but at my age I don't know if it would pay off. I don't mean in monetary terms, but in our present society I don't know if it would even get published.

For example, I have a terrible sneaking feeling that if Benét had turned in the manuscript of *John Brown's Body* last week, it would have a hard time finding publication. That may be unjustified cynicism, but I do know that another writer of very great prestige — a Pulitzer Prize winner, Robert Penn Warren — wrote a long epic poem that was published and went absolutely nowhere. We are just not a country geared for the appreciation of poetry.

Don't get me wrong. First of all, one thing I cannot abide is the sense that I'm writing something *to* myself, that I'm speaking to the world from a phone booth where the lines have been cut. At my age — and let's face it, you're speaking to an advanced septuagenarian — one doesn't have that option. It takes a great deal of strength and concentration and will, as well as talent, to write a major work. You can't go into it lightly.

If Armand Hammer came to me tomorrow and said, "My boy . . . ." He may be younger than I; but he could still say, "I would like to underwrite an epic poem, to be published no matter what. I don't care if nobody buys it, we'll print 10,000 copies." Then I would do it. At least it would have tangible, physical realization. But I don't want to scatter seeds on a windy day.

BELL: It has been too long since you've written a book of poetry.

CORWIN: Well, look at my last one. Sold maybe 1500 or 2000 copies. I'm glad I wrote it, but the average book of poetry published in this country sells around 500 copies. I think that MacLeish's high point was 1500, and he was an eminent poet.

BELL: Could you consider writing a poem-project for television or radio?

CORWIN: Of course, I've done that in the past.

BELL: Would that give you the needed impetus now?

CORWIN: Yes, but there are differences. It's awkward for me to accept an invitation to do something for a station whose studios and technical equipment are far short of network standards, or whose public is small and specialized. I remember a local station undertaking a massive production with great actors, and doing it live before a studio audience. I was told later by the producer that the station received one letter from its listening audience. One letter.

There's an adage in radio, or at least in network radio, that each letter represents 10,000 listeners. But *On a Note of Triumph* got 7000 letters, and even a program as quiet as *Untitled* would get a couple of hundred.

BELL: Do you thrive under pressure? Do you like the challenge of deadlines?

CORWIN: I respond to deadlines, but that is not to say that I like them. There's a little lyric to which Lyn Murray set music in *Radio Primer*. "A deadline is the one thing I abhor/Go away deadline and don't come back no more/A deadline is hungry, a deadline must be fed/Some day I'll get so mad I'll kill a deadline dead." That pretty much describes my occasional vexation with deadlines.

BELL: But there aren't very many, if any, old radio hands that could start something at all. At a station like KCRW they have the ability to go national on NPR. It just seems worth the time, even though the initial response would be smaller than what you are used to.

CORWIN: Let me say that anything worthwhile is worth doing. I am loath to find myself joining the horde who believe that numbers rule. That is one of the sicknesses of the electronic media. But it isn't an easy thing to make a choice as to how you dedicate what time remains, to what medium, and to what end. I have to weigh whether I want to write a series for KCRW, whether I want to write a book, a play, or rise to the challenge of writing a novel.

BELL: How much time in a week do you have to devote to your classwork at USC?

CORWIN: I teach one day a week.

BELL: You still teach at the Idyllwild School of Music and the Arts.

CORWIN: Yes, ISOMATA.

BELL: How is what you do there different from what you do at USC?

CORWIN: It's for a much more mature group of people. The median age in that course is forty.

BELL: So you take a more aesthetic bent at Idyllwild.

CORWIN: The work at Idyllwild is creative writing. The subject at USC, at least in this seminar, is criticism.

BELL: I suppose the injection of what you teach in creative writing, coming back to USC and teaching criticism, tends to make you assign your students more writing than others.

CORWIN: I don't know the methodology of other members of the faculty, having never sat in another class nor they in mine. The only gauge I have is the student evaluations, a routine at most universities. The answers are fed through a computer, and a chart is given to each participating professor. One question is, "How does this course compare with others you have taken?" On that, I'm happy to say, I've always rated very high. That's the only index I have.

BELL: When you have the first couple of weeks of class, what are your typical assignments?

CORWIN: I get my students to unfreeze themselves. My first assignments are almost calisthenic, trying and usually succeeding in the task of getting them to express themselves without the usual restraints. I doubt if my methods are original with me, but they are based on no system that I'm aware of, no external system. The title of this particular course is not fixed. It can be changed by either me or the university — at present it is "Specialized Reporting: The Arts."

That gives me, and the students, the license of reporting on various arts. Accommodated in this schedule are film, television, architecture, photography, the interview, and music. Very often it exposes the student to stimuli they have never experienced.

BELL: Are you a great believer in the power of taste?

CORWIN: Yes, I am, bearing in mind always that taste is insular, taste is variable — that one's own taste goes through many refinements and permutations and declensions.

I have a friend who annually sends me a perfectly taste-less Christmas card — vulgar and not above expressions like "shit" — which seems to me not the flavor of the season.

I am very much bothered by lapses of taste. Taste really is exercised every time that you put a word down. Certainly, were I writing fiction as novelists do routinely, I know that elements of taste would be even more important in the manipulation of character and in action.

BELL: Given that administrators cannot give exams in taste to incoming freshmen, is there a limit to what you can expect from your classes, as a whole, at USC?

CORWIN: Curious that you should mention the difficulty of examinations in taste. I don't give them that as such, but do, at the outset of my course, have them express preferences. "What are your least and most favorite" publications, art, music, literature — every area except politics, which is none of our business. I do that simply so that I can understand, have some insight into the proclivities of that student, and thus be able to help him along those lines.

BELL: Along the lines he has already found.

CORWIN: Yes, or if I feel that in the expression of his tastes, he is conspicuously lacking in something and could profit by exposure to that, then I approach it directly. I say, in effect, "You may find that you do like opera. Have you ever heard *Carmen*?"

Sometimes it opens up a whole new area of interest, one that can bring a person much pleasure in his life.

BELL: Is it ever resented?

CORWIN: Never. Mostly appreciated. I would say unanimously so, except that there are some kids who are just naturally quiet and never open their mouths. But those that do open their mouths say, "I never knew it was so much fun."

BELL: What is with the quiet kids?

CORWIN: Sometimes it's shyness, sometimes shallowness, sometimes insecurity. Usually it is a combination of insecurity and shyness which I try to overcome.

One of the ways that I have of overcoming it is to require that each one read his own things aloud. I believe that I establish an atmosphere of understanding that an audition or a judgment isn't going on. They profit by the example of each other, and there is engendered a kind of group morale which they and I find helpful.

BELL: How do you walk the line between judgment and the critical environment in which taste is important, the tension you've just described?

CORWIN: I've been lucky so far. Maybe I've been doing something right in the fact that it doesn't seem to have been a tightrope-walking maneuver. If there is a bit of hesitation at the outset, it soon disappears. I am quick to establish that I don't believe in the competitive nature of a class. When I make an assignment, I very often have an option for another subject, so you don't have the effect of ten or fifteen students competing with each other to see who can express themselves best on a given subject.

I tell them to perceive themselves as a board of editors, rather than students, to encourage openness. They're sitting around, and each one furnishes the other with a copy of his text, the author reading aloud, and we go around the table. I encourage editing for substance, for the handling of the subject, for color, even for typos and misspellings. "Page two, second paragraph, line three, what's wrong with that?" I never tell them what's wrong with it. They must discover it, and they do. They feel comfortable with each other quickly because they know that they're being treated alike and fairly.

I tell them that occasional misspellings will not count heavily; that Thomas Jefferson spelled very poorly. There are all kinds of instances of bad spelling in very high writing, but that isn't to say that you shouldn't spell correctly. Editors are not as charitable as I am, and you are going out into a world where you're competing, where the tidiness and correctness of your writing is salient and important. But don't worry that you'll get a "C" instead of a "B" because you misspelled four words in the text. I make it very clear at the outset that I don't believe in education by regurgitation, where they learn and then spill it all out in an exam to prove they read it.

I encourage the dissolving of the barrier between teacher and student. I may tell them about some conspicuous failure that I experienced around their age or even later. But at the same time, you have to keep a certain level of respect for competence. You have to be careful not to make it too lax, a snap course. I don't think they perceive it as such. They have too much work to do.

BELL: Do you think it's unfortunate that the young person can't join the world as you did at eighteen as a newspaperman and have twelve years before thirty, instead of eight or less?

CORWIN: I can't answer that too objectively because I often wonder whether I would have been better off had I gone to a good school rather than straight into newspaper work.

When I voice this, the most general reaction is that, "Oh, you were much better off doing what you did." But at the same time I have great respect for the discipline of *learning* — aside from the discipline of sheer hard work which was the discipline that I had to apply.

BELL: One thing that I've noticed in much of your early radio writing is your use of the rhetorical question, direct address; and you have certainly written some of the most famous instances of this in radio.

That mythical writer's manual will tell you to stay away from the rhetorical question. It begs an answer from someone not present and interferes with the normal discourse of the script.

CORWIN: I think that one should scrupulously stay away from those mythical writer's manuals and professors who feel that there is something suspect about the rhetorical question. It is ancient and honorable, and it appears in such marvelous sweeps of biblical language as, "What is man that Thou art mindful of him?"

What was good enough for Socrates is good enough for me. I love questions. They are the spirit of inquiry. Philosophically, the interrogation mark is perhaps the greatest single symbol of man's existence on this earth. We have nothing but enigmas and questions to ask about life, the universe, death, and even the cause and cure of the common cold. Questioning is the motive power, the engine, of our progress.

"How can we get this thing off the ground? How can we find a cure for cancer? How can we reach the Moon?"

BELL: In his book about radio playwriting, Max Wylie — who was story editor at CBS radio at one time — warns young writers against using your approach.

"Corwin, by the inclination of his style, wrote not of people but of Platonic individuals, disembodied, remote, symbolic . . . his rubrics and vignettes have not served to illuminate character nor to explore the emotional interior of a protagonist, instead they illuminate a mood."

CORWIN: To a degree, Wylie is correct in describing the thrust of my style, but I think it is an overstatement. Wylie was not that familiar with my work. It never went through him. He never passed on it, and he did not hear all of my programs. His judgment has been expressed elsewhere, and I do not find myself defensive about it. In the very nature of what I was attempting, I simply did not have occasion to do what Wylie says I did not do. But I think he was quite correct in advising young writers not to try to write as I did, providing — an important provision — that they wanted to write another kind of material, if they wanted to write soap operas or dramas or studies of character. Since the typical radio broadcast at that time was a half hour — minus opening and closing routines that cut it to twenty-seven minutes, of which some more would be lost to commercials — one could hardly enjoy Chekhovian depths of penetration.

But I don't want to sound defensive. I made my choice and lived with it. There are specimens I could cite that would indicate that I did not find character and development of character alien. I was simply too occupied with issues and with ideas as Wylie justly comments. I simply could not treat the broad murals that I was writing with the kind of patient and delicate detail that would go into a valid, worthwhile portrait of a character. I called upon myself to address historic and commemorative canvasses. I don't fault Wylie for writing what he did, but if he could have expanded upon it, treated it at greater length, he would have been under some compunction to footnote his comments.

BELL: If you had unbroken broadcast hours or 90-minute programs, would that have rebalanced your thinking?

CORWIN: I'm searching my memory for an answer to that. I have enormous respect for the writer or dramatist who penetrates character, who builds and molds his drama in personal terms — Arthur Miller, Tennessee Williams. The shelves are full of playwrights who have distinguished themselves in that area. I must come to the conclusion that I was attracted to a world of ideas and magnitudes that could not, in the time I had to prepare my work, enjoy the kinds of exploration — the psychological contouring of character — that is proper, indeed obligatory, in the writing of personalized drama.

There have been instances where I did have both the time and occasion to develop personal stories, to deal with characters, notably in *The Blue Veil*. I took characters who were originally rather stiff and elementary in the French script and developed them on my own. I felt and still feel pretty good about that and think that if that script had been seen by Wylie, he would have given that a footnote, surely. There's an analogy to be drawn by an analogy-draftsman, between the leitmotif in music and the use of symbols in plays which are committed to a program.

BELL: Is there any part of the phrase "symbolic drama" that gets under your skin when applied to your own work?

CORWIN: That term is too loosely applied. Hank Peters in *Untitled* is no mere symbol, though he may be representative. He's more than a symbol. Everything is symbolic in some sense. Our clothes, a kiss — all are symbolic.

BELL: Is consciousness of symbols and signs deadly to artistic verve?

CORWIN: If a symbol is static and exists only to act as a street sign, it has function but not interest. It strikes me that it is possible to construe Hank Peters as a symbol. He was a kind of guy that I knew. I had seen him in action, and I knew the people around him. The mother is a symbol. No mother likes to see her son walking down the street, off to war. Every mother would wonder what it's about. "Why did it have to happen to my boy?" That's a symbol, but it's no less human for it.

BELL: It's easier to see Hank Peters as a symbol when you look to the form of the presentation, *in absentia* until the end, described by others and revealed at the end to be the narrator, Fredric March.

CORWIN: That, of course, was a trick. Legitimate, but a trick nevertheless. The art of dramaturgy rests upon many pillars, and one of the tallest and stoutest is character. There is much in literature that derives principally from character. It can be great literature and often is. To the extent that the writer draws upon his own persona, he is autobiographical, and his characters are formed by his experiences, prejudices, attitudes. But a truly great artist can populate his works with people who are outside himself, be he Brueghel or Balzac. He evokes from his observation and his hearing — the acuteness of his hearing and vision and memory — a population for the stage upon which he tells his story. But those works, I submit to you, were accomplished in periods when there was not in existence, or yet dreamed of, electronic communication. The metabolism of broadcasting was such that it could not afford even what *The New Yorker* magazine affords — to subsidize a writer to go off for six months or a year, to get a profile, to study a story in depth. And I was committed to that metabolism — one that could not possibly have given me the luxury of contemplation, study, development, rethinking, and revision that is routine in the writing of a play or a novel.

BELL: There's a line in your television play *The Discovery* in which the leprechaun says, "The great ones are great because they have fought their way back to those staging grounds between light and darkness."

I submit to you that since light and darkness were so clearly and climactically struggling in the world in 1941, there was little need for you to have reached into your own recesses.

CORWIN: I think you've come nobly to my aid.

Chapter 12

BELL: You published one long poem in the 1960s, *Prayer for the 70s*. Do you find that poem detached today?

CORWIN: Well, I'm afraid that you have a misreading of the piece, at least one that varies from my own. This is in no way critical of your view, but it is not really a prayer. The term "prayer" is used in an ironic sense. It is a petition to man, not to God.

BELL: Wasn't it recast as a guide to man by the end of the poem?

CORWIN: No, not really. It can be read that way, and I'm pleased that you feel it could, because the intent, if you look at it again in the light of what I'm saying now, is entirely ironic. We know that God is not going to grant boons. In my view God — if there is a God, be he man, woman, black, white, or some kind of reaction between deuterium and lithium — is far too preoccupied to bother with the scrapings and squirmings on this very small planet of a second-rate star in an average-sized galaxy, one out of billions. I don't hold with the notion that God sees the fall of the sparrow. I don't think that God dictated the Ten Commandments to Moses — or if he did, he was certainly much rewritten.

I have many quarrels with the orthodox concepts of God all up and down the religions. If God were as majestic an entity as has been advertised in these religions, he wouldn't be vindictive. He wouldn't have to be praised and petted and adored and sacrificed to. He would be above that. He would be a compassionate God. He would not suffer little children to be cremated in airplanes blown up over the jungles of Burma.

I trust there is no element of piety in *Prayer for the 70s*.

BELL: When I used the word "detached," you used the conjunctive concept of "irony." As I recast the poem in my mind, God has gone away, but how is unclear.

CORWIN: I'm intrigued by your reaction, and I want to stake out the direction from which it came. I feel that it's a passionate poem, far from being sterile or removed. It says, in effect, that there *are* wonderful things.

There are profound and mysterious and quite marvelous things in the phenomena of life and death; all of them imply, it seems to me, the questions put to Job at the end of that great book. What do we know? We know very little.

It is as wrong to assume that there is no sense of universal order as it would be to assume that God has office hours eternally and that he is endlessly watchful.

You're looking at the book now, and let me help you. The mysteries involving time and the arching upward from the mud; the question of whether ours has not been a drunken course, not necessarily worth the trip; whether the mansion of existence has many windows; or whether it's just a big white elephant boarded up and haunted by our mistakes.

It was natural for you to think that this passage, the whole poem, holds an assertion that there is a God. It's an assertion that there are unsolvable mysteries — and I hope they remain that way. The text also appeals to man's instincts. "It means that the love of man and woman is a table of percentages, and their desire a disease of the id." Let it *not* be that. "It means that birth is a happening between pills." Let us *not* dismiss birth as routine and just something for demographics and the census.

"And old age a phase held together by plastic parts." Let us make sure that it is *not* just that.

"Death is a package deal with the best advertised mortuary" is social criticism, for too often it *is* that way. The next line says explicitly, "So God, if you are alive/and in that heaven we have come to know/is spotty with systems of gravity/each pulling for itself. . . ."

The operative word is *if*, isn't it? "Then perhaps you must flex the muscle of divine authority."

That doesn't claim that God is in his heaven. That doesn't turn to Revelations chapter and verse.

BELL: But "If" and "Perhaps" lead you down a path of thought that has implications that God *is* who you are addressing *if* He or It is there to be addressed.

CORWIN: Not seriously. This is a prayer to man, not to God. As I said before, how do we know that, when the phone rings on God's desk, he will pick up the receiver?

Good God man, there are ballplayers who cross themselves when they come up to the plate. The coach of the Notre Dame football team crossed himself three times before the kickoff of his first game against Michigan State.

Is anyone claiming that God favors Clemson over Auburn?

Absolutely ridiculous. We should not be so blasphemous as to charge God with that kind of petty concern.

BELL: Don't they cover their tracks by saying that they are praying that everyone plays well and no one gets hurt?

CORWIN: Why should God say, "You pray to me, John Jones, therefore you will not fracture your femur and this other guy, who did not pray, can break his ass." Let's face it, we have to elevate our sights.

We talked earlier about the relationship between listening interest and statistical returns. *Prayer for the 70s* was written at the instance and urging — rather insistent because I was rather busy at the time, and I resisted — of Eddie Albert. He was going to appear on *The Ed Sullivan Show* for Thanksgiving and wanted me to write a prayer. This piece was my response to that.

Now, if it was antiseptic, as you started to say, if it was, well, *neutral* — why did it get 30,000 letters? That's more than I got for *On a Note of Triumph*. Why did it get all that mail? People writing in to ask for copies of it — why? The then-editor of the *U.S. News and World Report* called me up and wanted to run it in that publication.

BELL: If I had to guess, it would come down to the last five verses, beginning with "That being the case, dear busy God/please manifest thyself again through one superlative new-minted covenant/create for the lot of us/all nations indivisible/an act of God more stupendous/than the mere parting of waters/or a standing sun . . . ."

CORWIN: Isn't it ironic to say that treating a man decently and not discriminating against him because of sex or color is a staggering miracle, greater than the parting of the Red Sea?

BELL: Yes, it's ironic, but considering the sentiments of this country at the time you wrote those lines, it was not necessarily to be taken ironically.

Didn't you get letters telling you what a wrenching and true prayer you wrote?

CORWIN: Yes, but I think they were praising its sentiment. I think in that sense you are vindicated in your view of it as a prayer. You tell me it's a prayer, a legitimate and straight prayer to God. Apparently those 30,000 people thought so too. That was not my intention, but I'm pleased that it got that reaction. It meant that people listened to it, for God's sake.

It's not a gross misreading. It's only *honi soit qui bon y pense*. Whatever anyone wants to think it is, that's fine by me.

BELL: How did Eddie Albert read it on *Ed Sullivan*?

CORWIN: Your way.

BELL: Really? Did you instruct him otherwise?

CORWIN: I wasn't there. However, he should never, never have looked up to heaven as he spoke it.

BELL: By the 1970s, due to changes in political art or philosophy, the audience as a whole, or a much larger fragment than previously, was accepting the kind of imagery that you used in *Prayer for the 70s* — straight. The audience in 1970 was conditioned to the workings of the systems, doom and hollowness, to accept this as reality while still wanting the sugar-coating, the reassuring payoff. Ironic or not, you gave them sugar at the end of this piece.

CORWIN: I don't think so. I disagree. At the very closing, it flings a challenge at man.

BELL: "Long past time to act."

CORWIN: Damn right. It says, "Look, it's serious now. It's very late."

It's a lot to ask, but I'm addressing man. "Look you. You'd better feel decent about your kind in all his skins and pigments and stop killing. That's asking a lot, and it *would* be a miracle, but it's getting late, long past time to ask."

It was interpreted by those thousands — who may represent a few millions — as being directed, that's right, toward the heavens. But it really is asking miracles of *man*. I would not compromise the piece, torpedo it, by explaining in a footnote, prologue, or epilogue that I really don't think God is the one to talk to about this. Talk to yourself, talk to your congressman, talk to your neighbor.

BELL: But if you're going to stage this poem, don't you have to make absolutely sure that the reader directs himself to the audience during the last stanzas.

CORWIN: I'm not being fair to Eddie Albert when I say that he looked to heaven. He did look up once or twice, but not in the last lines, I must say. That would have been totally unforgivable and would have destroyed it. Even if he had looked up during a preposition, that would have been one time too many.

BELL: What was your state of mind when you were writing the poems that comprise *Overkill and Megalove*? There is a lot of bile in that book, by your lights.

CORWIN: That was a hard book to get started on. Again I was *asked* to write, had my arm twisted by the editor in chief of World Publishing. I found the contemplation of the atom bomb and what it had done so distasteful to me that I approached it with a sense of nausea.

But I got over that. Feeling depressed when I began the book, and unable to get off the ground with it, I decided that I would lay aside what I was doing and get on a ship. I asked my travel agent to nominate some freighter upon which I could sail away. He did, and I went down to Panama. The peace on that ship, the sense of being cradled in the deep, had a tonic effect on me. I overcame my depression and started on the book. Once I got started, all the toxins in me seemed to be neutralized.

BELL: Do you have favorites in the book?

CORWIN: Let me say I have no dislikes in the book, which is unusual for me. I pretty much stand by what I wrote and how I wrote it. If I had it to do over again, I don't think I would change much.

There are a couple of pieces that are slighter than others, but I think that's a form of relief.

BELL: Some are merely epigrams, part of a structure of a ten-part poem of snippets.

CORWIN: Oh, those are parodies.

BELL: Some were, I knew, but were they all?

CORWIN: Let me see. The parodies are in a section called *A Fireside Album of Familiar Verse*. The first one parodizes a poem by Dickinson; the second a poem by Vachel Lindsay;

the third Sandburg; the fourth is A. E. Houseman — "with
rue my heart is laden . . . ." The fifth is Edna St. Vincent Mil-
lay; the sixth is Keats; the seventh is Robert Frost; the eighth
is T. S. Eliot; the ninth is Kipling; the tenth is Coleridge —
Kubla Khan. All parodies.

BELL: You were honing your penchant for moving logic —
in this case from the *grosse* — prefacing nearly all of your
poems with either a quote from a philosopher or, more
generally, some piece off the wires of the *Associated Press*.
    Was that an easy principle to arrive at in the concept of
the book, taking the large logic and breaking it into its
premises?

CORWIN: Yes, but that's hardly novel. It acknowledges the
takeoff point and is useful in orienting the reader. In an
entirely different milieu and spirit, S. J. Perelman would
also do that, would take some sentence or two from a
personal ad or a want ad and run with it, to hilarious effect.
In a way, it also serves the purpose of establishing the
currency of the subject. It was in the press and a subject of
general concern.

BELL: Do you draw the line between art and didacticism?

CORWIN: There is a very clear line between the two. I feel
that, in my less inspired moments, I have blurred that line. I
regret that.
    I think that didacticism is a pejorative term, and I hope
that even when I have blurred the line, I have not been
overly didactic in so doing.

BELL: Do you have a preferred term?

CORWIN: I can comfortably accept the term, "socially conscious writer" — addressing myself to societal matters. In doing that, I am in good company. What is *The Grapes of Wrath*, but that kind of a work? Some of the poems of Shelley and much of Shakespeare deal with humanity and its follies and problems, with the arrogance of power, the excesses of venality, human nature.

BELL: This is from a poem in *Overkill and Megalove* called *Now, About That Next War, Son*. You quote a line that you had originally written many years before for Paul Robeson to speak — "Now we're in it together . . . ."

CORWIN: It's more than a line that I quoted. Much of that earlier piece has been reused in this.

BELL: How do you respond to the assumption that nuclear weapons have prevented the next war for these last forty years, which takes that very sentiment as its core — "we are all in it together"?

CORWIN: The answer to that is two words — so far. That has not been very long. The menace is irreversible.

We are, at the moment of this discussion, a few days away from a summit conference to limit armaments, which is another form of proof that this is a continuing menace, and that it is constantly on the minds of the powers large and small.

BELL: If you had ended *Prayer for the 70s* by substituting the lines that you ended this poem with — quite the same surface sentiment — do you think that you would have gotten the letters?

"Tell him the choice rests in the care of what fragile peace we have, including his trusteeship, if he but live to his majority. One or nothing, wealth or laying waste; Jew and Gentile; men or the color of men. These are the choices, and we make them daily. Tell him he must learn to answer for himself." This certainly would not be called *ironic*.

Is the choice of irony a difficult one to make when determining the approach to a piece?

CORWIN: Not for me. Irony is present in almost everything I've written, but there's no great trick in being ironic or perceiving it.

BELL: Not including *Could Be*, which was produced years earlier, how long did it take you to write the poems comprising this book?

CORWIN: Not very long. I never write in a straight line saying, "Well, I'm going to lock myself in a room and do nothing else." There were social engagements and lectures and other things that intervened. If one were to put together the actual working hours spent on it, it would come down to no more than six weeks. Or even less than that.

BELL: Have any of these been reprinted more than others?

CORWIN: I don't think so. There wasn't much of that.

BELL: It seems that at this time your metrical concerns were minimal, well illustrated in this way by *Landscape Before Crashing*.

CORWIN: Meter comes naturally to me. I never slave much over it. It is a form of breathing for me, never a struggle. In fact, even when I have written in formal rhyming verse, it does not come hard.

That is not to say that there are not hang-ups and certain isolated cases where I am not satisfied and rework it; but going on a long-term basis, averaging out those lines, I have never been conscious of it being onerous or troublesome.

BELL: *Landscape Before Crashing* is such a powerful metaphor it would seem to beg for dramatization of some kind.

CORWIN: It's interesting that you should say that because, not appearing on the records anywhere, it was dramatized on two occasions.

One was Studs Terkel doing it for a group in Chicago and broadcasting it — with my permission, of course. The other was when I was one of the board of directors of a theatre group out here which took up its residence at a theatre on the RKO lot, which had become the Desilu lot. The theatre was made available through the largesse of Lucille Ball. As a project for the company of actors that belonged to this group — a non-profit organization — I adapted *Overkill and Megalove*.

That turned out to be a formidable project, quite satisfying to me and to the other people. It enlisted a lot of good actors and the music of the late Joseph and Miranda Marais, folksingers and composers. They did the score, and some of the pieces in the book were set to music, like the piece entitled *Exceptions* — "Brother, we are brothers all ... ." That one was marvelously done by them. There's a poem about insects taking over, and they had a great musical treatment of that.

BELL: What was cut from the book?

CORWIN: About half. I'll give you a very fast and painless synopsis of my approach.

The characters were the faculty of a college. I wrote a lot of new material for the framework. The faculty was introduced at the beginning of what was to be a semester. It fills up a bleachers onstage, and the interlocutor — the president of the college or the registrar — announces the courses and each professor steps out and does his thing. Thus, the professor on astronomy did the moon poem, and the professor on theology did *Cosmonautica*, "When reached for comment, God said . . . ." We had a lot of fun with that — God then coming on to speak his piece, raising and lowering the lights by merely moving his hands. Let there be light.

But as I said, there is no real record of this production. The play was not open to the public, hence not reviewed by the press, except for a notice in the *Hollywood Citizen News* whose reviewer had been sneaked in by a friend. He wrote a smashing review, a rave.

BELL: It was never publicly performed?

CORWIN: No. It only had three or four performances. It was really an in-house exercise.

BELL: One social angle that I found interesting was your seeming opposition to the space program at the time that you were writing *Overkill and Megalove*. Was there some philosophical disagreement there?

CORWIN: To this day I believe we should explore inner space before we explore outer space. The problems that we have on the crust of this globe are so overwhelming that we can indefinitely postpone those adventures.

I am as thrilled as anybody by space accomplishments. I have to say that from an idealistic point of view, it's marvelous that science has achieved what it has done and is continuing to do. I am a cheerleader for those photographs taken by the space probes of the outer planets. But I read now that they are talking about a space platform for the 1990s that will cost billions of dollars. I want to see the homeless taken care of before we take care of space technology, at a time when social services are being cut back and are in danger of even more cuts in the near future. It is wanton and irresponsible, and it approaches disgrace to consider spending billions on space hardware for no immediate, practical purpose. The principal generator of interest and activity in that kind of space program is military, and we have so many military problems without extending them into space — that what we could gain scientifically or militarily from such an adventure would not be worth it.

Maybe when the millennia arrives and we have universal disarmament and a world at peace, then all nations could contribute to this in the spirit of *Could Be*.

BELL: Did you ever meet your fellow Bostonian, who institutionalized space exploration, John Kennedy?

CORWIN: Kennedy was the one president whom I knew and dealt with. I actually directed him in the recording of his narration for a script that I wrote, half of the keynote speech at a political convention. That's a story in itself, the year that Kefauver ran for Vice-President when Jack Kennedy was still Senator.

I was asked by Dore Schary to write a film for the Democratic National Convention, that film to constitute half of the keynote presentation at that convention, the other half being a speech by Governor Clements of Tennessee. I wrote that script, and Dore asked me for notions as to who would read it, and it required a solid narrator.

"It just so happens that I'm having lunch with Ed Murrow tomorrow," I said. "He's in town, and I'll ask him. He's much closer to the kind of awareness that a question like that requires."

The next day at lunch I told Ed about the film, and he thought for a while. He tossed out the name of John Winant of New Hampshire — who had a good, Lincolnian face — and one or two others. Then he arrived with a eureka snap of the fingers at the name of John F. Kennedy. That struck me as a good idea, too. I reported this to Schary. Schary set in motion the necessary inquiries through the Democratic National Committee — a cinch to do — and Kennedy agreed to do it.

He came out to California to do it. We had dinner at Schary's. Kennedy went over the script with me, very deferential and polite, and he had very few suggestions for alteration. He liked it. I remember one of his reservations was an allusion to his father which he thought would not be very productive in the light of his father's many enemies.

BELL: Just a simple allusion?

CORWIN: Yes, that was easily remedied.

Then, after about page 3 of this 30-page script, he closed it, and we proceeded to have a very nice evening.

A few days later we filmed it at the Goldwyn Studios on Santa Monica Boulevard, one of those sound stages there.

I've forgotten who filmed it. I directed it — in the sense that I worked with Kennedy on the reading, and he asked for my input. That was a memorable couple of hours.

This was not the end of the historic interest in that film. When that film went on — and keep in mind that it was fifty percent of the keynote address — CBS chose not to carry it and cut away from it to some inconsequential convention-floor interviews. Paul Butler, who was chairman of the Democratic National Committee, raised hell about it, to no avail.

BELL: Did CBS provide a rationale for that?

CORWIN: A lame one, as I remember.

They had the right to cut away. It's a question of whether what they substituted had as much interest. In a sense it was inexcusable in that responsible people had put it together. It was a worthy film. It dealt largely with a very concentrated history of the Democratic Party. Running through it was a good deal of information and a cohesive presentation of Democratic ideals.

BELL: It would have nothing to do with the fact that it was from your pen.

CORWIN: No, I don't believe so. I took no credit on the air for that, so that couldn't have been it.

BELL: Nor Mr. Schary?

CORWIN: I don't think so.

BELL: You never met Kennedy again?

CORWIN: I did meet him again after he was nominated years later for the Presidency. There was a big reception at the Biltmore, and I was invited by someone to go down. There were a lot of people standing on line. I thought, "Christ, he'll never remember me with all these people."

He was receiving, and when he got to me his face brightened and he said, "Well, well, Norman it's good to see you." Here was a guy — of all the people that he had been in contact with over the years, he still had a memory for a face and a name.

There was another contact after he became President, in his first two hundred days or so. There was a friend of mine, a fervent Kennedy supporter, who had been helpful in the logistical arrangements for the convention film. He was dying of cancer. On the quiet, I wrote to Kennedy and suggested that a letter from Jack would bring him considerable cheer. By God, he wrote that letter. That was my last contact with him.

I liked him personally very much, but I was disappointed after his death when the disclosures came out regarding his acts of commission and omission in the Vietnam war.

I thought that Johnson ruined a chance to be a truly great President by his tragic obsession with Vietnam. I felt that his social programs were remarkable, and that not since FDR had we had so much progress in that area. We are indebted to him for that. Indeed, as I look back over recent Presidents, I have to agree with those who believe that Nixon earned himself a merit badge in history with the *rapprochement* with China. It was historic and very important.

As with Johnson and the monomania over Vietnam, Nixon spoiled the act for himself, if not in other ways, by Watergate. That was one of a series of American tragedies.

Reagan is a tragedy all by himself.

And the list of American tragedies must include that of Jimmy Carter and the hostages in Iran, when he blundered into playing generous host to the Shah and got the Iranians down on him. He could have been returned to a second term if not for that, I'm pretty sure.

BELL: It seems to me, in the light of the beliefs and actions of my generation, it wasn't so much the radicalization of the young in the '60s that shakes us today — the idea that some kind of rapid revolutionary change *might* be worthwhile in America — but that so little lasting change was effected by it.

CORWIN: The history of all nations is one of a series of causes and effects. I think that every radical movement, if it succeeds or runs out of steam because certain adjustments are made, suffers a kind of complacency. "We've won that objective, and it's all over." Like the feeling that I personally had after World War II. "That settles that. Now the future's going to be bright. We and our blood brothers in war will be good friends now that we've destroyed the horrible monster."

The return to the TV set and Disneyland, after a period of taking to the streets, is not unexpected. It describes the normal trajectory in social issues. It is only when people suffer, can take it no longer, or are spurred by an event or a charismatic leader — or the interaction of the two — that they become radicalized. Hunger will radicalize; unemployment will radicalize; fighting a senseless war and beginning to realize it after the rhetoric has run aground; having terrible inequities — the blacks and the poor mostly fighting a war and getting killed. All that will radicalize.

I'm using the term "radicalize" very loosely here. Simply because one takes action doesn't make him radical.

Radicalism in this country is a pejorative term. We do not allow, ever, that Washington and Jefferson and Hancock were radicals. Oh no, no, no, no — they were pure, patriotic, one hundred percent Americans. They wouldn't have gotten on very well with the Un-British Activities Committee at the time, and didn't.

As long as a man is employed, has got a paycheck and a job and can feed his kids, can come home and watch football and drink a beer — he's not going to worry about the homeless of Scranton, Pennsylvania. He's not going to worry about our squandering our money in Haiti or Chile. He couldn't care less about those things. He'll return to office whoever was holding office at the time when he was enjoying this modest prosperity. But the minute he's out of a job and his kids are hungry or his son has been drafted to fight in Indonesia in a war he doesn't give a shit about, he will take a different stance, both on the streets and in the elections.

BELL: Is there a sense in your mind, looking back on that period with an eye to your thesis of trivialization — was this a particularly fertile and profound time for this, for political trivialization?

CORWIN: Yes. My concern is that, thanks to the electronic media, particularly television, and thanks to the forces that now engage us — trivialization is accelerating and moves on a broader front. It trickles down into areas that it had not reached before and has become endemic.

We lose sight of our values, trivialize our values — perhaps the most dangerous of all forms of trivialization.

BELL: It seems that in all of the talk we've had about the subject, we seem to be circling the duality of whether democracy is a revolutionary process or a reactionary one.

CORWIN: Anything can be subverted. As I tried to point out in some passage or another in some play or other — church bells have been melted down to make cannon, and the electricity that lights cities is also used to execute men. So can democracy be used to ill effect, abused.

Nevertheless, when you look over the vast landscape of political systems that are in place today, my feeling is that wherever the people — as a viable constituency — have the power of the plebiscite, yes or no, wherever they can make a choice, the course is far safer than in the denial of that. In denial you are placing your faith and trust and hopes in a benign oligarchy or aristocracy or some system like communism or fascism. Whether it be a triumvirate, a troika, a dictator, *glasnost*, or Peronism — it is not the will of the people.

The people can be wrong, sometimes resoundingly wrong. But given all the other factors that are fed into the computer upon asking this question — when it is a question of making a choice that will affect issues of war and peace, their own lives, and well- being — the people will come up with a better choice than the one imposed on them.

As we speak, two days from the end of 1987, I have a feeling that the people of Israel may not approve of what their government is doing in the Gaza Strip. I know that the people in Chile would not approve of what is happening in that country, and that the people of Haiti do not approve of what is going on there.

My worry about the so-called enlightened countries, of which we rightly consider ourselves to be in the vanguard, is that they are being and may continue to be subject to the pressures of mediocritization and trivialization. I make a sweeping bow in the direction of television for responsibility, and not one of respect. If one were to go by percentages, like a baseball manager, the percentages favor democracy — economic and social and cultural. Most of the vitamin group is in democracy.

BELL: Are there more things to react against and upon in America today?

Is there a choice *not* to react remaining?

CORWIN: I don't think that we are being softened by TV sets or comfortable lounge chairs or well-upholstered automobiles. There is nothing wrong with any medium as such — radio, television, the press. It is what is *done* with the medium, how those media are manipulated. The responsibility rests first with the gatekeepers — the producers and entrepreneurs — and ultimately with the men in top positions. The public isn't taking over the television studios and wouldn't know what to do with them if they did. The men and women who are running the great engines of information and entertainment must educate themselves to a kind of morality that is now very rarely found among them. The slavish reliance on ratings is a long-festering sore. The almost automatic exclusion of quality is another thing that has to be addressed. Then, of course, it goes back to the school, what is being taught. I'm an outsider, without benefit of any pedagogic training, but if I might say for myself — and I will since no one else can — that many of the comments from students in my class are of the order of, "For the first time I feel as if I'm being educated." That's one hell of a comment, but not so much on me as on the rest of the curriculum. This statement could be construed as terribly self-aggrandizing, but there it is. I have to be honest with you. It's a pity if maverick or exploratory or experimental or intuitive or any combination of those approaches are so few. Is it because the bureaucratic structure is so heavy?

BELL: Does it seem, at this time in your life, that your long, hard pursuit has accomplished what you'd hoped for?

CORWIN: It is sometimes melancholy to look back over the years to the advocacies to which I lent my energies and to realize that I'm either at square one or in some minus position. Not I personally, but the kind of national outlook that I was speaking of.

BELL: What is your sense of responsibility today?

CORWIN: Responsibility is well and good, but you only have one life to live and only a limited number of hours in which to live it. I cannot espouse every cause in which I believe, seek to forward it or support it in writing or any other way. I have to be selective.

If I won that $25,000,000 lottery that was announced yesterday, my greatest joy would be sitting down and writing checks for $500 and $1000 and $5000, sending them here and there and answering the mail that I sadly have to sift and throw most away. I'd love to be able to support everything. I don't mean some erratic Don Quixote approach to this, but there are lots of things worthy of support. I'd also like to buy a new car and a nice house for myself, instead of renting an expensive apartment.

I stand exactly where I stood fifty years ago. I don't mean to say that I'm standing still but that the commonly acknowledged virtues of decency and humanity and honesty and justice and equity don't change with the season. Those things, to the extent that I have embraced them and been of service to them, have not changed. Politics and government have changed, modes and fashions have changed, but the verities that trace back to the first recorded musings of man on these subjects, remain the same. The great concerns of moral distinction have been constant since the Hammurabic and Mosaic codes, all up through every variation on those themes.

But I don't think life is balanced anymore. It is tilted and has been for some time and is in grave danger of capsizing. Not only the obvious and palpable dangers of chemical and thermonuclear war, of baleful scientific techniques that can be activated at any time including 3 o'clock this afternoon; but in the quality of life, in the fact that we have not begun to be adequately prepared to cope with the second greatest danger to the area we live in, the overdue earthquake that threatens to destroy our city.

And all you have to do is get in a car on a Sunday — or during any one of the 12-hour-long rush hours — to realize that more and more high rises go up, the population increases, the cities expand into megalopoli. There are fewer jobs, more poverty. We are consuming our physical world at a dreadful rate, cutting down even the forests of equatorial South America; and over no distant span of years, we may begin to suffer the consequences of carbon dioxide pollution, the greenhouse effect, the loss of our protective layer of ozone. All these are terribly erosive and corrosive effects. I'm close to the end of my life, but I'm sorry for young people, people as young as you and younger, who are going to have to cope with this increasingly as the years pass, unless something very concrete is done about it *soon* — a program of international cooperation, the prospect of which is not yet in sight.

BELL: Arch Oboler wrote a play, just before the end of World War II, called *The Day the Sun Exploded*. It was about the meeting of nations on a very clear day in which they all signed intentions never to fight war again. Just as they put their pens to paper, the sun explodes, signalling the end of the play.

CORWIN: I do not subscribe to that kind of fantasy, including the invasion from Mars in *War of the Worlds* because that's *deus ex machina* in spades, a calling upon unrealistic outside forces.

Much more important, I think, is a play like *The Day After* or the movie *Testament*. Those, to me, are much more persuasive and valuable. The other is really, in a way, entertainment for grown-up kids. It has its uses and is entertaining or horrifying and scary. Irony, by itself, is of small value. We can't do anything about the sun blowing up, but we can do plenty about the menaces and problems that I catalogued a moment ago.

BELL: Have you been interested in science fiction and how it has liberated fiction for many people?

CORWIN: I don't feel that the science fiction revolution was all that revolutionary, nor do I think it had a particular liberating function, in that there was excellent science fiction written long ago, going back to Jules Verne and H. G. Wells. Let's face it, the one science fiction story that made a great stir in the history of broadcasting was a piece by Wells.

It did please me, though, that fantasy became more marketable and available. In that sense, your use of the term "liberating" is justified.

If you speak of "fantasy" as against "science fiction," then I dealt with it early, and with pleasure — *My Client Curley* and *The Odyssey of Runyon Jones, Descent of the Gods, L'Affaire Gumpert, The Plot to Overthrow Christmas.*

I never came close to the degree of absorption with either fantasy or science fiction that either my friend Ray Bradbury or the late Arch Oboler did.

BELL: If you were going to write a broadcast next week on a subject of science, what would you write about?

CORWIN: I have always found the sciences intriguing. It was wistful appreciation since very early I discovered that I had no proclivity whatever for the mathematical arts. I barely scraped through math and couldn't deliver an algebraic equation of the simplest kind if my life depended on it.

Nevertheless, I've been a fan and spectator of the vast and — to me — romantic, poetic cycloramas of astronomy and medicine, of electronics. But the uses made of science for destructive ends — in *Holes in a Stained Glass Window* there is a text of a lecture that I gave at the University of North Carolina some years ago in which I go into that.

I am hostile to the study of war, in the sense of that marvelous spiritual, "We Ain't Gonna Study War No More." I am hostile to that study in science, too.

BELL: If dramatic radio had been allowed to proceed for another ten years, what might have happened to the form and content?

CORWIN: I can only speak about what might have happened to my kind of radio. I have no idea what would have happened to the soap opera — perhaps nothing — or of what would have happened to serious music or to comedy. They were going along pretty well. They were successful, and there was no reason to seek mutations or "improvements" in them. But the one area in which there might have been development was in my own — that is to say, the treatment of radio as literature, as dramaturgy to be taken seriously, as a form of documentation with an identity of its own.

I dare say there would have been more writers like myself coming along and, I have no doubt, better ones. Had I remained, I would have improved along with the field, along with the technical advances in sound and engineering. There would have been more resourceful and daring use of sound, even though in my time I was given credit for representing some of the best of the state of that art.

When I measure the distance between the best sound then and what we have today, it makes me sad to think that none of that was available — nothing of today's quality of sound, today's microphonic techniques and equipment.

BELL: Did you think of yourself as a creative, imaginative writer or as a sociologist or documentarian?

CORWIN: The former, definitely. The sociological approach, my documentary activity and such, were an accident. We had a war on, and there were burning issues, and I was among those burned. I felt strongly, and that feeling showed in my work. Not that I would have been without social awareness had there been no situation of war. Were it not for issues that, in a sense, demanded the services of my kind of radio man — and I'm speaking of war programs, the *American in England*, the *Bill of Rights Show* in 1941 — I would have written a great deal more personal drama, comedies, more poetry laced with music. The ratio between that kind of writing and production and the documentary and socially oriented would have been altered.

BELL: So, it's after the war, and radio has ten more years, and the issues change. Did the drama of the issues have to change?

CORWIN: Not the drama, but the urgency. The drama of the issues never changes. The issues are always with us in one form or another. Not necessarily war, but all of the dynamics of society, domestic and foreign, are constant.

Chapter 13

BELL: Tell me something about the *Group W* television series.

CORWIN: The series *Norman Corwin Presents* came about as the direct result of the prime-time access fight. For anybody browsing through these notes who is not immediately aware of what that entailed, it was the claim by independent broadcasting entities that they were being discriminated against by networks, closed out because of a kind of monopolistic hold that the networks had over their available time. The fight was led by Westinghouse Group W and one or two others. They demanded that they have a share of prime-time, that they have access to the important hours of prime-time broadcasting. Radio, I believe, did not figure in this at all. It was too unimportant, relatively speaking.

The proponents of prime-time access won. Now it was incumbent upon Westinghouse Group W, which had the production facilities and apparatus, to furnish programming once they had won the fight. At the same time that they invited me to do this series, they invited the Smothers Brothers, Mal Sharpe, and some other people; and we all went on the air through Group W's limited channels, limited because Group W had access only to its own O&O stations which numbered five or six in very good areas —

Boston, Pittsburgh, Baltimore, Philadelphia, San Francisco
— but not Los Angeles, curiously enough.

They tried to sell these productions on a syndicated basis
to other stations and got very little response since eighty or
ninety percent of the broadcasting industry was in a
dudgeon because Westinghouse had won. They were quite
content to go along with the *status quo ante bellum*. The
series, however, was carried by the entire Canadian
Broadcasting Corporation's network.

It was decided to produce the series in Toronto because
the difference between production costs anywhere in the
States — especially on the west coast — and costs in
Toronto was very great. Sufficiently so that it paid the
operation to be based in Toronto, even though the entire
staff, including myself, were on expense accounts, were put
up and fed and transported; even though we had to import
our stars and pay for their transportation and lodging and
expenses and meals, to say nothing of the fees — which
themselves were higher because the people were travelling
long distances — being based in Canada was an economy.

BELL: So you used Canadian crews.

CORWIN: They had to be for the series to qualify for
broadcast over the Canadian Broadcasting Corporation.
They had to have what they called "Canadian content" —
that is to say Canadian writers, actors, and the entire
technical staff outside of those we brought with us.

We used some Canadian directors. I imported Ted Post,
among other directors, and I directed some myself. Each
program was done in one week with little lead time, which
tended to be used up quickly. We used a platoon system.
One show preparing and one rehearsing. It was put

together with extraordinary dedication and hard work and with an extraordinarily small budget.

BELL: Who is Ted Post?

CORWIN: Ted Post is an American director who for years directed the long-running soap opera — written by a woman in New Hampshire — *Peyton Place*. He also received many kudos for *Go Tell It to the Spartans*, starring Burt Lancaster, a Vietnam-war film which, in the view of many, was among the best of the Vietnam-era movies.

BELL: Who was Arthur Joel Katz?

CORWIN: A lawyer-turned-producer whom I engaged as a line producer.

BELL: How many shows were produced?

CORWIN: Twenty-six.

BELL: How many out of that lot did you write solely, not direct?

CORWIN: I wrote seven of the episodes and directed probably five of the seven. I was artistic director of the series, chose the scripts, and had veto power over all decisions.

BELL: Your art director's name on that show was Robert Rappaport. Was he a Canadian?

CORWIN: No, he was an American — ex-Philadelphia I believe. I don't know what became of him after the series, but I was very happy with his work.

BELL: They were certainly '60s set designs and colors. Everything was very bright and flat.

CORWIN: Yes, that's right. Bear in mind, however, that these were remarkably low-budget shows. It was for budgetary reasons that we went to Canada in the first place.

BELL: Did you conceive it as a series of more or less single-set shows — two or three at the most — shot entirely in the studio?

CORWIN: That was never a dominant factor in our decisions. We were economy-minded when it came to sets, nothing elaborate, but a number of the programs, a half-dozen I can think of offhand, had multiple sets.

BELL: Did you utilize the bluescreen on programs other than *The Odyssey of Runyon Jones* episode that I saw?

CORWIN: Maybe once or twice.

BELL: I'll tell you the shows that I've seen, and you can give me any thoughts you have about them.
   The D.J., which was written by M. Charles Cohen.

CORWIN: Yes, a Canadian.

BELL: Was this the only show Arthur Joel Katz directed?

CORWIN: He directed one other that I can remember.

BELL: What attracted you to this script, aside from its small cast and set?

CORWIN: It was good writing and an interesting look at a D.J. — tightly written. It was also, I felt, beautifully performed by Frank Converse. He seems to me one of those talents who — like some others I can think of, one of them being Monte Markham — are persistently underrated.

BELL: Was the opening dialogue-less sequence in the script — his awakening and getting to the studio and his pre-show operations in the studio before he gets the phone call from his wife?

CORWIN: That was all scripted.

BELL: *Letter from an Only Child* starred Diane Baker and was directed by Charles Dubin from a script by Don Balluck. Again, a show that didn't seem to have much to do with you.

CORWIN: It didn't. That was a program of middling quality, I felt, although Balluck is a very fine writer, one of the best. He was represented by another program in the series called *Aunt Dorothy's Playroom*. That had far more puissance, although if I had written or directed it, I would have made changes.

BELL: That program also starred Diane Baker.

CORWIN: Yes. *Aunt Dorothy's Playroom* is an allegory pure and simple, which dealt ingeniously with Ralph Waldo

Emerson. It had a great deal to say about our values and our society and did it in a way that enlisted the best qualities of Bob Rappaport. I thought Balluck was quite inventive in that script. It bears reviving.

BELL: A show that you wrote and directed was called *Jefferson's Crush* with Lloyd Bochner as Jefferson. If you had an unlimited amount of money to remake that episode, how would you change things?

CORWIN: Unlimited amounts of money always make a difference, except for instances such as *They Fly Through the Air*, which had a very modest budget, as did some of the other programs that registered high on the Beaufort scale. It didn't need a big budget.

In the case of *Jefferson's Crush*, one could have enjoyed a richer tapestry. I give that program a "B" or "B minus." I did not consider the woman who played Maria to be optimum casting, a Canadian actress, especially considering that the original Maria Cosway was an extremely beautiful and delicate woman whose portraits have come down to us. Not that one should evaluate an actress on a cosmetic scale, the way critic John Simon is so quick to do.

That program retreats from memory with more speed than others. I don't have a particularly warm recollection of it.

BELL: You seem to be trying to draw a strong point in that script based upon the difference in type from the attraction of Jefferson's intelligence and that of Maria's beauty.

CORWIN: I confess I don't have theories about that. I feel that what a man or woman finds attractive in the opposite sex is a zone of mystery. I have seen many weird alliances over the years, and wondered sometimes about my own — what a woman would see in me or I in a particular woman.

However, I felt there were very few liberties required in writing that teleplay, since it was explicitly spelled out by Jefferson himself. He was an exceptionally articulate man. The spine — if not the last dotted *i* and crossed *t* of that script — was there in Jefferson's famous letter to Maria. Perhaps it isn't that famous, because when I discovered it in a relatively obscure volume, I was delighted and astonished to find there was such a document from this dignified statesman.

BELL: That letter begins and ends the play.

Two of the shows were adaptations of your own radio scripts. The first was *The One Man Group*, an adaptation of the *Gumpert* script, and the other was *The Moat Farm Murder*, which was directed by Lela Swift. What can you tell me about her?

CORWIN: I thought the directors uniformly, with one or two minor exceptions, were quite gifted and operated inventively within the limitations of these productions. I realize now that there are several scripts and tapes that I don't possess. I don't have *Reunion* or *The Moat Farm Murder*.

I do have *The One Man Group*, though. Donald Herron is another talent that, I feel, is much underappreciated. I have a feeling that if he and Converse were working in England, they would have high stature.

BELL: In *The One Man Group* you had Gumpert's wife meeting a psychiatrist on an airplane, then telling him the story of her husband, rather than just telling the story directly to the audience as you did on radio. Why?

CORWIN: I never approached my problems from the standpoint of "what is necessary," but from a sense of what would interest the viewer. Pace, balance, a solid launching, and a variety of backgrounds are what I'm looking at. It seemed that the device of having the psychiatrist a prisoner, a captive audience on that plane, was a perfect device. It avoided the relatively drab, straightforward narrative which was too often inevitable in radio. But even if I had thought of that device in radio, it would have been effective.

BELL: The radio script contained much more movement, flights from scene to scene.

CORWIN: Sure, but the main ones were in the TV version — Carnegie Hall and the rest. Gumpert became Paganini, then an 18th-Century Alsatian kleptomaniac, then a Yorkshire farmhand, then Freud.

BELL: Steve Binder, who directed this program, is best known for his big musical revue shows of the '60s. How did he come to your attention?

CORWIN: Most of the directors, with the exception of Ted Post and Jeff Hayden, were the suggestions of Joel Katz. I discovered an interesting thing about Binder when he worked for us — that Mrs. Binder is distantly related to me, so Steve is one of the family. I like Steve's work, and I think he's a very gifted director, a joy to work with.

BELL: The three programs that I saw that were written and directed by yourself were: *The Discovery* with William Shatner, *The First Big Try* with narration by Donald Sutherland, *Soliloquy for Television* with Brock Peters as the

Soliloquist. *Two Gods on Prime Time* was directed by Binder in a talk-show format from your script.

CORWIN: Yes, but I also thought that a couple of the best programs that you haven't mentioned yet were *The Undecided Molecule* and *Crown of Rags*, the latter not my script. Those are two of the best.

BELL: Have you ever read Brecht, his ideas on staging?

CORWIN: No.

BELL: Would the staging of something like *The Pursuit*, so unconventional in approach, have changed much if you had a few million to do it?

CORWIN: I don't think so. *The Pursuit* took place in limbo, and I think limbo is an attractive ambiance for fantasy. This was a kind of fantasy that — although it dealt with reality, the Vietnam war and the grinding-down of the individual by taxation and bureaucracy — was symbolic. The symbols are not remote at all. They are meant to be quite clear. Allegory is fine, as long as the consumer does not have to descend in a bathysphere or dynamite his way through hills of granite. *The Pursuit*, both in its concept and production, was stock. That was its intention. But perhaps I'm part answering and part anticipating what you might be asking. I know what conditions you are applying — your allusion to Brecht.

Actually, in terms of direction and especially in terms of staging, I am not able to trace influences. It is largely intuitive because, unlike my writing which has clear influences which I can trace, I am not indebted to Brecht or anyone else. I didn't see their work, being relatively undereducated in theatre. I've seen a lot of movies, of course, hundreds of them; but in terms of actually staging my own things, neither the legitimate stage work that I've done or the television work is particularly indebted to anyone.

BELL: In the *26 by Corwin* series with House Jameson as the soliloquist, you wrote *Soliloquy to Balance the Budget*. Since I haven't read the script, I must ask if this could be considered something of an examination of radio as *Soliloquy for Television* could be considered an examination of that medium?

CORWIN: There was much less of that in the radio version because, being a visual medium, television had so much more to offer. It has an eye, and you can dramatize an eye — what it sees, and how it itself appears. You cannot do that with an ear.

BELL: Do you keep a joke file or a notebook of reasonably subjective things to say for use in your scripts at a later time?

CORWIN: I don't keep notebooks, and that saddens me very much because I have respect for those writers who do and the salutary results that come from that. Chekhov is a great example.

BELL: Do you remember the circumstances under which you wrote *Soliloquy for Television*?

CORWIN: I had approached Stan Freberg to write an original, and unfortunately he never did, but he led me to expect that he would. When the deadline approached and there was no script from Freberg, I had to fill the gap. As a matter of fact, two other undelivered scripts resulted in programs — those being *The Pursuit* and *The Undecided Molecule*, which Katz did not think particularly funny and did not want to include in the series. He later acknowledged he was wrong when a tape of the program was played before an audience at the Glen Glenn Studio, and the room rocked with sustained laughter.

BELL: That was the only one before an audience?

CORWIN: That one, and *The Pursuit* as well. The laughter was general, and the audience was not children. Charles Champlin and Cecil Smith were there and enjoyed themselves, and I must say in fairness to Joel that he was very charming about his acknowledgment after that program was over. He had a right not to think something funny.

BELL: Who referred Brock Peters to you for the role in *Soliloquy*?

CORWIN: Joel Katz and I went over the casting together, considering available people who could make it to Toronto. I may have even said, "Hey, I'd like to get a black actor for this." Generally, there was agreement on casting.

BELL: What was the time lag between completion of script and shooting?

CORWIN: Very little lead time at any stage.

BELL: There were references to the color of the soliloquist's skin in the script. I was wondering if those were conceived after the casting of Peters.

CORWIN: I don't recall adding anything for Peters. I probably knew in advance that he would do it.

BELL: Were you satisfied with the quality of acting in that series, overall?

CORWIN: I found it generally acceptable, at times better than that. There were two or three percent that were failures.

BELL: You only wrote one adaptation yourself, *The Blue Hotel*?

CORWIN: It may have been the only one, yes. *The Blue Hotel* had been strongly recommended by Ted Post. I was not familiar with the story, but I read it and liked it very much.

It must be said that later, a year or two after that series was done, one of the major networks made a prime-time adaptation of *The Blue Hotel* with stars, though I've forgotten who they were. I had very few opportunities to measure the quality of my own series so precisely against a program of a similar format. Mine were 26-minute programs. Tuning in, I thought, "Now I'm going to get some lessons on how this should be done." To my happy surprise I realized that our *Blue Hotel* was much superior to theirs, better directed by Herb Roland; and Leslie Nielsen was very good indeed in the leading role. The character actors were all great. It came together with great force.

BELL: What was the origin of the script *The Discovery*?

CORWIN: That was an adaptation of *The Hyphen*, a stage play that I did for the University of Utah to inaugurate a new campus theatre there. Bill Shatner came to Salt Lake, rehearsed for two weeks, and played it for two weeks. I believe we've already spoken of that.

I later adapted it and called it originally *Fairy 589* and then *The Discovery*. The title of *The Hyphen* comes out of a speech in the play referring to the hyphen between dream and reality.

BELL: Did you feel confident in the editing room on these shows?

CORWIN: I was in the editing room for every show with my cutter. The scripts were tightly and economically written, never much hassle between the shooting requirements and the requirements of the editing room. In other words, we never had big, sweaty problems — more often a case of trimming down to minutes and seconds.

BELL: Were there any other attempts at documentary, other than *The First Big Try*?

CORWIN: I'll get the scripts out and see. I see a pair of love stories here. *Jefferson's Crush* being one, and *The Better It Is, the Worse It Is*, a very poignant story, the other.

The First Big Try seems to be the only documentary. We got our footage from the United Nations for that.

BELL: Sol Saks wrote a script for you, directed by Ted Post called *Bingo Twice a Week*.

CORWIN: Let me see. Yes, he did write that.

BELL: Another script having a political, humanistic tack was called *A Son Come Home*, with Georg Stanford Brown, written by Ed Bolens and directed by Charles S. Dubin.

CORWIN: I remember that vaguely, not very well. It was perhaps one of the two or three programs in the series that I liked least.

BELL: *Please No Flowers* was written by Joel Ensana and directed by Peter Boretski, two names I noticed nowhere else.

CORWIN: Peter Boretski was an actor who also directed. I believe he plays the psychoanalyst in *The Discovery*.

BELL: Tell me about your relations with Group W.

CORWIN: Group W, represented by George Moynihan, was wonderfully liberal and permissive. When they decided, after the original thirteen weeks, that they would renew, they made only one request — to have more programs of black interest. This was refreshing, considering the history of minority representation in television. I suspect the interest was largely conditioned by the fact that their stations in Baltimore, Philadelphia, and Pittsburgh were watched by blacks more than by any other group. This was never expressed to me in those terms, however.

BELL: Where is Mr. Moynihan today?

CORWIN: Still with Group W. In fact, it is through the bounty of Mr. Moynihan that you were able to view any of the tapes, as he was generous enough to give me copies of the shows.

BELL: It was about this time that you were writing your play, *Cervantes*, as well.

CORWIN: Not simultaneously.

BELL: Was that something that you had planned for a long time?

CORWIN: Not at all, not at all. Alas, this was commissioned rather than something that I wanted to do on my own. A producer in New York, whose name I have forgotten at this moment, had made arrangements with Richard Kiley to play Cervantes and with Frank Corsaro to direct it. This, of course, was subsequent to Kiley's great success in *Man of La Mancha*.

BELL: Did you have enough time to write it well?

CORWIN: I had enough time to write it. It wasn't done under the kind of pressure that had gone into every one of my radio and television series. And I researched it rather carefully, the research being difficult in that relatively little is known about the life of Cervantes. Nobody even knows where he is buried. He left very little biographical material behind him. This was not about Cervantes' characters but about Cervantes.

The play opened at the L'Enfant Plaza Theatre in Washington, D.C., to generally hostile notices. But there were dissenters from that, and I remember a letter to the *Washington Post* from Rod MacLeish — nephew of Archibald and a news commentator from CBS — who had seen it and wrote indignantly to the *Post*, protesting what he thought an unfair review.

The thrust of the criticism was levelled largely at Corsaro, but that would have been unfair because I was there and could have made strong representations had I differed with Corsaro to any great extent. We did have differences, though never unfriendly.

I did some work on the script after it opened, and I must say parenthetically that it opened without benefit of previews — always a mistake. The opening was hurried in order to accommodate a date for the theatre.

Cervantes toured the country and did a lot better outside. It wound up collecting some decent reviews. I don't think it made much money, and I don't think it lost much money. It was a play that passed in the night as far as I'm concerned.

BELL: You shot the Group W series on video. Was there anything ever shot on film?

CORWIN: No.

BELL: After working on radio for so long, were you satisfied with television stage sound?

CORWIN: The burden of sound in any visual medium is far less than in radio where sound compensates for the absence of vision and visual information. To that extent, the use of sound requires less imagination on the part of the viewer. Accordingly, in the feedback process it requires less inspiration, less poetic positioning in approach, in the thinking of the writer.

BELL: But it still has to sound right, not hollow or tinny.

CORWIN: It was always adequate for the needs. The Toronto facilities were very fine, equal — except in editing techniques which were a little slow arriving in the Dominion — in camera and sound techniques to the best of what could be had in this country. Naturally there had to be a less ambitious prospectus than if it had been underwritten by a network with a budget several times greater than our operation.

But then, that was right in line with the entire history of my productions — not "entire," as there were periods circa *On a Note of Triumph* and *26 by Corwin* when CBS was not stinting.

Let me remind you that my first series for CBS was called *Words Without Music* — that being controlled by the fact that we didn't have a budget for music. I never approached my scripts for radio from the standpoint of wanting to spend a lot of money — as though if I had twice the budget, the show would be twice as good. There was never a significant correlation between the effect and the budget.

Now, of course, that ratio diminishes in a visual medium. *Cry Freedom* would not have been the canvas that it is without a lot of money. Certainly special-effects films require big budgets. But the line stops this side of radio.

BELL: As of this sitting, when was the last time that you were on a set or a stage?

CORWIN: The last time I was in a control room — and then only in a kind of advisory capacity — was when Walter Cronkite performed my piece, *Network at Fifty*, on CBS's 50th anniversary.

BELL: How did you get involved in that?

CORWIN: Alex Cohen, a first-class Broadway producer whose TV specialty was commemorative galas and award shows, was engaged by CBS to create a week-long celebration of the network's jubilee. One afternoon, early in the preparation of what amounted to a mammoth mural, Alex and Oscar Katz — the latter representing the top brass of CBS — came to see me at my digs in West Los Angeles. They invited me to write an ode to be performed as the end-piece of a stretched-out retrospective — six nights of nostalgia totalling fourteen or sixteen hours of prime time. I accepted and wrote a piece called *Network at Fifty*, the text of which would run about nine or ten minutes. I proposed that it be read by Orson Welles, but it turned out that Orson had already been reserved by NBC for its 50th anniversary show, which came in the same year. I then suggested William Holden, whom I had come to know, and whom I admired as a superb actor. But Bill had a very bad throat ailment. Then Alex got the notion of dividing my text among seven stars who were already engaged to appear in other segments of the week-long program. They were Lauren Bacall, Alan Alda, Mary Tyler Moore, Carroll O'Connor, Walter Cronkite, Cicely Tyson, and Eric Sevareid. Glamorous as that lineup might be, I didn't think it would work because it would mean seven different styles, paces, timbres, and stances — one following the other. Alex decided to give it a chance to work. Each of those good people separately worked up a portion of the ode, and each was taped, to be presented consecutively on the air. It did not work. Alex and I agreed that the best reading had been that of Cronkite, so he was given the whole text.

BELL: Were there effects or music used to back the poem?

CORWIN: No sound, but an original score was composed by Leonard Bernstein. It was written as background, and I don't think it could be called, nor was intended to be, vintage Bernstein.

BELL: Has the text of *Network at Fifty* ever been published?

CORWIN: Yes, in a handsome but too-limited edition of fifty copies, brought out by Ward Ritchie, a printer-publisher eminent in his field. The edition, now a collector's item that is hard to come by, enjoys a preface by the late novelist and poet, Robert Nathan. It's a very beautiful and moving short piece, and that's all I will tell you about it.

BELL: *Network at Fifty* has such scope — involving past through the present flung into the future — and is so definitive a commemoration of the network's half century; one has to wonder why CBS didn't think to publish it as a special edition of its own, as they did with *Seems Radio Is Here to Stay*, much earlier.

CORWIN: Ah, a different crew was on the bridge. Had Lewis or Coulter or Kesten or Stanton been in command, had the wise old first lieutenants like Bill Fineshriber and Davidson Taylor still been in uniform — perhaps the network would have made something special of that text. It still serves, and will hold for the 75th anniversary, although of course I won't.

BELL: Wasn't there some talk of a CBS 60th anniversary show?

CORWIN: Yes, and I was to be in it as one of the four or five featured people in the network's history, as a matter of fact. There were many hours of research on graphics, a hundred period photos of myself in action, pictures of myself with my casts, my stars, and so on. But the Writers Guild strike of 1988 came along, and I understand that the project, after having spent well over a hundred grand, was canceled by none other than Lawrence Tisch. *Sic transit gloria* 60th anniversary.

BELL: In the late 1940s, when you left CBS, were you contacted by NBC regarding your services?

CORWIN: Not once.

BELL: Do you find that surprising?

CORWIN: No, because I thought NBC dragged its feet, was timid and unimaginative, and that it found men like Murrow and me not particularly cut to their style. It was the difference between a Paley at the helm and a Sarnoff, or you name him.

After all, consider what happened when Bill Paley got ready to raid NBC — and cleaned them out of Jack Benny and other stars of the moment. You never heard of NBC raiding CBS. I felt that, in that era, NBC was overshadowed by its parent, RCA.

Chapter 14

BELL: I know that you've been heading committees for the Academy of Motion Picture Arts and Sciences for a long time. How did you get so involved in Academy matters?

CORWIN: I became a member of the Academy when my screenplay for *Lust for Life* was nominated. Through the interest and offices of the late William Gordon, who was a PR guru at Universal for many years, I became a member of the Documentary Awards Committee. I had not been on the committee but a year or two when some issue came up in which I took a position opposing a policy that I felt was undemocratic.

BELL: In the selection procedure?

CORWIN: I've forgotten exactly what the issue was, but I think that it dealt with "undue influence." The force of my statement, which I recall as being well expressed, came to the attention of Margaret Herrick who was then executive director of the Academy. It was she who tendered the invitation to me to succeed Preston Ames, who up to then had been the chairman of the committee.

So here I was, a freshman, entrusted with the chairmanship of that committee. That began a long association, now around twenty years, with a hiatus for my times in Canada.

I've had the privilege of contributing to an improvement of the status of the documentary film within the Academy structure.

BELL: That must give you satisfaction.

CORWIN: It does.

At the time I took over the chairmanship, the nominations of both short documentaries and feature documentaries were compounded to form a tenable evening, or program, to be shown to the full membership of the Academy in deciding who would win the Oscar. If we nominated, as we did one year, a 3-hour feature-length documentary, we had time for only another 30-minute short.

Otherwise we would be out of bounds. We couldn't keep people in that theatre all day or night. And each film was shown only once and voted upon by direct ballot at that meeting.

I felt that this was unfair, demeaning to the documentary film. All other pictures were shown twice and were not limited by considerations of "what will make a program."

That was one of the first stands that I took — using the pronoun "I" — quite aware that the committee had to approve any action taken, but I was nevertheless the author of the language and the concept. My resolution went up to the Board of Governors and was approved.

That was one of a series of perhaps ten adjustments over the years that I like to think have done a great deal to assert and maintain the integrity of the documentary.

BELL: Can you elaborate on any of the other adjustments?

CORWIN: Yes, I can. I led the fight to prevent the documentary from being elbowed out of the annual Award proceedings. Fairly recently there was a movement underway to give the documentary awards on a separate evening, along with the scientific and technical awards. There would be a dinner; and the winners would then be filmed in a tightly edited form and run on the show, rather than the nominees — ten of them all together, five short and five feature-length — being present in the theatre like all the other members of the population of nominees.

This narrowed down to a rather hotly contested issue, brought before the Board of Governors. There was a lot of pressure in support of the proposed change because every year the Awards show would run past midnight in the East, and they were trying desperately to find ways to cut that down.

My argument, among others, was that if you make cuts, cut some of the music, cut persiflage, but don't cut out the one area where, without question, the most serious social issues on film are dealt with.

BELL: Not to mention the fact that these are the films that need that publicity the most of all the nominees.

CORWIN: Exactly. I made a pretty strong case for it. It would be unseemly of me to register the approval that I received from my fellow members of the Board. I managed, let me say, pushing modesty aside, to reverse a preliminary vote by the Rules Committee of 11-2 in favor of the change to a vote by the Board of Governors of something like 28-3 against it. I felt pretty good about that for a full twenty-four hours.

BELL: You don't think that this is something that will have to be fought again?

CORWIN: It may. "Ever" is a long time. But in future it will be harder to make the change, thanks to the minutes of that meeting.

BELL: So, you presided over the committee the year that *Hearts and Minds* won the award, by far the most controversial documentary Oscar ever.

CORWIN: Of course, you realize that the committee only nominated that film.

BELL: It was impossible not to nominate.

CORWIN: I felt that way, and so did the committee. I must say that the chairman does not ever, at least this chairman, try to influence the committee through his office. He may make a statement, but when it comes to an individual picture, I would never use my chairmanship as leverage.

BELL: Does the committee, or a sizable portion of it, have a political agenda for nominations — or attempt balance of some sort?

CORWIN: No, they really don't. The membership of the committee represents mixed political affiliations and mixed points of view.

BELL: Do you feel that most of the best documentaries of any year happen to be politically correct?

CORWIN: Yes, I think so, but the term "politically," in the sense that you have just used it, risks being pejorative, just as the term "politician" on its face is pejorative.

BELL: I mean it to be a bit pejorative. But to take it at its broadest level, a film like *Masters of Disaster* is not political. A film like *Chile: Hasta Cuándo?* is political.

CORWIN: One of the criteria, and perhaps the most important in this day of a perilous world, is the importance of a film. We come back to that word.

There can be a very beautifully-made film about the flora and fauna of the estuary of a river in France. There was such a film made, impeccably, but if it is in competition with a film like *Chile: Hasta Cuándo?* — which was necessarily crude, shot covertly, and has deficiencies in terms of grainy film and sometimes diffused sound — there can be no comparison. I daresay that in the judgment of the Academy membership at large, that is concurred in.

Another thing about criteria — the purely entertaining film, and there have been some marvelously entertaining documentaries, also faces what may be an unfair competition with pictures of very serious social moment.

BELL: That's interesting. Is it an unfairness that needs to be combatted?

CORWIN: No, I don't think so.

Because of the elements that come together in the expression of a popular vote on any work of art, many and complex, it would be fruitless to say, "What are we to do about the fact that a picture about the violation of the rights of American Indians won out over a very entertaining picture about buck-and-wing dancing?" Such pictures were nominated, but if you are to put it on that level, it cannot be reduced to "What are we going to do about this?"

The only thing to do is to judge pictures as objectively and honestly as we can, allowing ultimately the heart to enter the equation along with the head.

BELL: Were you surprised at the victory of *Hearts and Minds*?

CORWIN: I was not surprised that it won.

BELL: The assertion was made in the press that it was a propaganda film.

CORWIN: That question could only have been raised by extreme partisans of the war itself, by those who felt that the war, and our role in it, was impeccable and beyond challenge.

It was, by all odds, the most unpopular war we ever fought, and this was a film that polemically addressed that. It was done with great force and great skill.

Again, I must remind whoever is reading this that the judgment to nominate is made by forty people in a screening room, but the award of the Oscar is made by four or five thousand members of the Academy at large, representing perhaps a greater percentage of Republicans than Democrats.

BELL: But mechanically that is not necessarily so. Correct me if I'm wrong, but the right to vote on the short documentaries at least is limited to those present at screenings. Doesn't that apply to features, too?

CORWIN: The award to *Hearts and Minds* was made before that rule went into effect.

BELL: What do you think about that rule?

CORWIN: I think that it's an excellent rule, and it should be applied to every film shown.

BELL: Do you get a great number of entrants in the Documentary Short category, compared to Feature?

CORWIN: About the same number, but of course the screening takes much less time. I think that there were around seventy entries this year.

BELL: What are generally the best kinds of subjects to devote yourself to in a documentary short?

CORWIN: The documentary short explores far more widely than the feature. It costs less to do so. It can take up relatively small areas of human activity and thought. Therefore, there tends to be this wider range. Whereas a feature film usually interests itself in some issue or broad survey of whatever it is surveying. A short can be sometimes slight and capricious. Not that many are, but there are some every year.

I have a great deal of respect for the maker of the short because it is a form that promises very little in reward. Who is going to buy it, and who is going to exhibit it?

A feature is now down to sixty to ninety minutes for television, but we have 16-minute shorts, 20-minute shorts. Most of them run a half hour, but the maker of that film will be lucky to get his money back. My respect for them is high on the level of enterprise.

BELL: It might seem the category of the half-hour-or-less non-fiction piece is most and best done by television. Is the entrant in the documentary award this year required to state whether it was shot in video and then transferred to film?

CORWIN: No, the only stipulations are when it was made; where it was first shown; and whether it is eligible under the rather complicated system of qualifying through a recognized international film festival.

BELL: Has video been changing the scale of the things you are seeing or the way they are shot?

CORWIN: Definitely so, yes.
    For one thing, the improvements in remote photography, not studio-based, and the improvements in the cameras and techniques of ad-lib, *al fresco* shooting, have greatly freed the documentary filmmaker wherever those elements are useful.
    Television, for all of its shortcomings, has been the best friend of the documentary.

BELL: It continues to be?

CORWIN: I see no danger that it will dry up, though there will be periods of retrenchment whenever a network finds itself economizing.

BELL: Are you still co-chairman of the Scholarship Committee?

CORWIN: No, I'm not. I found that being on the Board of Governors and being the chairman of the Documentary

Committee and on the Rules Committee was too much. I have not been for some years.

The Scholarship Committee was conceived as an earnest enterprise, and it is in place to help worthy and needy fellow entities to underwrite their programs, programs that are in want of support.

BELL: What is the average Board of Governors meeting like?

CORWIN: The Board meets once a month, and sometimes there are special meetings. There are all kinds of things that come to bear — policies or questions like the one about the documentary's place on the main awards stage; questions of eligibility; questions of improper use of the Oscar as a symbol; questions of where the Awards show will be held; questions of support for the library; questions dealing with the physical plant of the Academy or the staff; with budgets; with special programs of films; programs to honor people like Johnny Mercer, as happened recently, or Fredric March; questions of screening policies. There is never a want of material for an agenda.

BELL: How is the Academy doing financially?

CORWIN: I think it's doing quite well. They receive a very good fee for the awards show itself, and membership at $200 a year is important revenue. And they have special occasions, fundraisers — not deliberately to raise funds but along the way they do. It is more than solvent, but you realize that the Academy has another arm called the Academy Foundation, of which I am presently secretary.

BELL: Who is the president of the Foundation?

CORWIN: Fay Kanin, past president of the Academy itself. She's constantly busy. There are very few writers in the industry who are as prolific.

BELL: Is there a fair distribution, do you think, of the professions and crafts within the Academy?

CORWIN: I think the Academy bends over backward to be fair. In fact, there are categories I've always wondered about, such as the category of "Members at Large."

BELL: Is that honorary, or does it have something to do with absence from production?

CORWIN: You catch me on a day where I cannot answer that. I don't know. If you would have asked me that last week, it would also have been a day that I didn't know.

BELL: Are you planning on staying with the Academy and USC for many more years?

CORWIN: I'm making no plans. I'm just hoping that I'll be around many more years. It begins there. If I were to embark on any serious writing project, I might take a sabbatical both from the university and Academy work.

The Academy work is not all that demanding, and my schedule at the university is not either, relatively speaking. There are professors who have two or three classes a week. I have but one and have kept it to that. But if some publisher wanted some work from me or made an arrangement for a long-term serious work, if *Trivializing America* had come along now instead of four or five years ago, I think I'd take the time off. I did that book in addition to everything else, and that was a big undertaking.

BELL: If something happened to *Trivializing America*, like a television limited series, would you be anxious to get back into that subject matter again?

CORWIN: No, I would do it only if there was some compelling reason to do so. Walter Cronkite has been very much interested in doing a television series based upon it. He would do it tomorrow if we had the funding.

BELL: Does he want to write it?

CORWIN: No, he wants to translate it to television. I would want him to. I have enormous respect for Cronkite and would completely trust him. I would certainly want to be close to him in the operation. If I could be of service to the realization of this as a TV series, I would do so very happily.

BELL: I've heard that you don't care for the technical requirements of television direction, but you've had a great deal of experience with actors. Have you considered co-directing television with someone who would handle that end?

CORWIN: I would be amenable to that because my interest is, as you have rightly deduced, in the *sense* of the piece, in values and interpretation rather than in the movement of camera and other aspects. Not that I am uninterested in that. My scripts are always conscious of the camera.

Very often when I'm in rehearsal and I feel that there's something wrong, some misstep, or some angle that does a disservice to the scene — I'll suggest a change; but largely the act of sitting there and calling shots doesn't particularly interest me. I would rather have that done by somebody much more amenable to the mechanisms.

BELL: Given that, do you ever participate in colloquia at USC or with acting and directing classes there?

CORWIN: I could, and the subject does interest me. I don't consider myself in the slightest sense superior to it. But my emphasis in teaching has always been on writing rather than on directing.

I feel that there are far more competent and gifted directors in the world than there are competent and gifted writers.

If I were these days to write a screenplay or teleplay and had the opportunity to direct it myself, I think that I would opt to do what you described in your question — to work with the actors and in the blocking; but I would be much happier if someone competent upon whom I could rely, and whom I respect, could take care of the rest. There are many such people.

BELL: Was there a point in your career when you thought of yourself as much a director as a writer, or were you always first a writer?

CORWIN: I always considered myself a writer because I began as a writer. Not only as a newspaperman, but when I got into broadcasting.

No — I take that back. I began as a director in broadcasting, at least in network broadcasting.

To the extent that my early work dealt with scripts by other writers and not of my own, I identified myself as a director; but then the functions were grafted on each other. For the rest of my career in radio, the functions were unified. I wrote for myself as director and directed for myself as writer and produced for both.

BELL: In listening to either old broadcasts or new, what is most often missed in the average script or broadcast that could have made it a better play?

CORWIN: There is no one thing, I think; but a lot depends on a sense of taste, an ear for rhythm, and a feeling for the unity of a piece. Of course, many elements contribute: casting, atmosphere, sound, the integration of music. It is hard to isolate a single factor, unless there is a conspicuous lack of it that cannot be avoided in judging a piece.

Most of radio — and for that matter much of what is being written for theatre and film — lacks a sense of importance. Not that this is a requirement, and certainly the term "importance" is subject to many interpretations, but this is perhaps, to me, best exemplified by a script that was sent me this past week by a writer who had done a script for the *Westinghouse Group W* series.

I had directed the script, and David McCallum had starred in it. It was called *Crown of Rags* and was written by Howard Brown. He sent me a script that he has just written for the theatre. It was a competent script, and he wanted my thoughts on it. I told him that it was fine, but I thought that it was unimportant, whereas *Crown of Rags* had a great deal to say and a great deal of himself in it.

I just yesterday got a letter from him, thanking me and explaining what had induced him, motivated him, to write that particular script. He did not disagree with me, but was simply explaining. What makes something important and another unimportant depends first upon the artistry with which it is done, secondly on the subject matter. *The Bicycle*

Thief was a small but very deep, honest picture, and it didn't set out with a naked agenda.

BELL: In your own work for radio, you often set yourself up with an expansive, formal allegory that expressed itself in language that was common and straightforward, aggressively toward both sides of that equation.

CORWIN: The   degree   to   which   language   appears colloquial depends on where we are and where the language is coming from. Nothing today could be more colloquial than the hundred instances, and that's a conservative figure, in which Shakespearian or biblical language is part of everyday, common speech. Most people are unaware of this even as they use the phrases. Some things in the Bible are as colloquial as "Howwaya kid."

Basically, colloquialism — which has nothing to do with vulgarity or incorrectness but relates to language that is not on a formal level; familiar, conversational language — is independent of era. Try these on for size: "The apple of his eye," or "Be of good cheer." "A man after his own heart," or "Fight the good fight." What about "At the point of death," or "For ever and ever," or "In the twinkling of an eye"? All of these expressions are around today, all are current, all much in use, all are colloquialisms of long standing. Yet every one of them comes straight from the Bible.

And let's not forget Shakespeare's colloquialisms — colloquial today to the point of being cliché: "You have to give the devil his due," and "Sweets to the sweet." "It was Greek to me," and "He eats me out of house and home." There is "Dead as a doornail," and "I'll tell the world," and "It smells to heaven." All were colloquial in Shakespeare's time, although they were not yet cliché, having just been minted.

As to the colloquial in my own writing — which now and then appear among passages we have agreed to call "heightened language" — I never use them in the sense of saying, "Well, that's a pretty highfalutin metaphor I've just discharged. I'd better have something to bring it down to earth." No, I just write as it strikes me. I think I am a creature of my time and of the language of my era, just as Chaucer was of his time and Marlowe was of his. I don't mean to make any grand comparisons, but it's convenient.

Also, I have a good model, in my view. One of the great strengths of Carl Sandburg was his use of the colloquial. Having known Carl better than I've known any other eminent writer, I know that he came by that faculty the same way I came by mine — not to be used for effect, but as the shortest distance between intention and expression.

BELL: If the shortest distance is a goal, then rhythm is critical to you.

CORWIN: That is the unstudied, instinctive element of the ear — whether you have a musical ear or do not. I think that I do.

BELL: In your book *Holes in a Stained Glass Window*, there is a poem called *Jerusalem Printout*. What was the origin of that piece?

CORWIN: In the early 1970s there was set up a week-long exposition at the Convention Center in Los Angeles called Jerusalem Fair. There was a replica of a section of the wall at Jerusalem built within the Convention Center. It was, I think, perhaps the first major exhibition of Israeli products and art in this country.

I was approached by the cultural attaché of the Israeli consulate here and asked if I would write the keynote for that. To kick it off on a ceremonial opening night, which included a Mormon choir — not the Tabernacle, I don't think — and the Mayor of San Francisco, the Mayor of Los Angeles, and the Mayor of Jerusalem. There were 2000 or 2500 people packed into that big auditorium. I was asked not only to write this piece but to deliver it.

I must now describe the effect of it since you ask about it. There was an enormous platform in the hall, no curtains, just a bare platform as big as the stage at the Shrine Auditorium, it seemed to me. I did the piece, and when I was descending the stairs after the long walk off of the platform, Teddy Kollek, the Mayor of Jerusalem, came forward and embraced me. He said he had been very much moved by it.

BELL: How did you conceive of the computer printout device?

CORWIN: I despaired of having agreed to write the piece. Wearily, I approached it and tussled with it and nothing came. I had spent all of six hours in Jerusalem, and that did not entitle me to write a book about it, or even a poem.

So I went to the history books, photographs and texts of Jerusalem. At first I was bored with it and shrank from the prospect and was on the verge of calling up and saying, "I'm sorry. I spoke too hastily. I've made some passes at it and can't get a line on it." Then, as I read, I became more and more interested in the subject. I realized how much I did not know about the history of Jerusalem. I can't recall what triggered the notion of the computer, but it was happy for me. As you notice in the piece, there are some deliberate glitches, things are deliberately out of sequence and are corrected.

BELL: I thought that you went to the books and then saw yourself as this organizing process came to life.

CORWIN: It works this way — you lay out what you have, all out on the table, and then you begin to try to create order from chaos. I had a similar problem with the structure of *A/777* where I finally settled on the roll call.

BELL: What are the qualities you would want to be remembered by in your writing?

CORWIN: The dominant emotion, I think, when not being ironic, was compassion and humor. In my best moments there was a kind of exultation.

A distinguished art collector saw a tape of a reading of *Jerusalem Printout* that I did for a local cable service, using Group W facilities. This woman called me and said that she thought the piece was "noble." She was the second one to use that word to describe it. What I suppose she was alluding to was that quality in my work that others have perceived as having a certain Olympian perspective, riding high over the scene — the literal position of the narrator in *They Fly Through the Air* — looking down, not with condescension, but with compassion, sometimes with bitterness, but the bitterness is an outgrowth of the compassion. For example, while we are compassionate toward victims of the Holocaust, we are also bitter and angry toward the authors of the Holocaust. It's awkward to defend oneself and to use such self-aggrandizing adjectives as "noble" and "compassionate."

BELL: You mentioned that these qualities are dominant when you are not being ironic.

CORWIN: I love irony, I must say. I feel like Luke Skywalker wielding his laser sword. The weapon is something I love to use, but I don't think I can be charged with using it improperly. I hoped to use it effectively against those deserving of it when I chose to. I do not have in my psyche any oasis of tranquility when it comes to the brutality and savagery of Pinochet, Idi Amin, Hitler, Stalin, and their ilk.

BELL: You once wrote a memo to the brass at CBS saying, in effect, we cannot be too squeamish about our enemies.

CORWIN: Oh yes, I think I actually said that at a conference at Ohio University, at the Institute of Education by Radio.

BELL: Is the enemy so pervasive now that, if you cannot be a little squeamish, you are likely to cut off your nose to spite your face?

CORWIN: You mustn't take a phrase like "squeamish about our enemies" and extend it. I'm not speaking of napalm or the H-bomb or My Lai. Indeed, in reviewing the history of warfare, the shedding of blood has never been prettier in one epoch than in another. There have been instances in which conflict has been gallant, has been chivalric, "noble" if you will. In the early history of New Zealand, the British — who had no business being there — were fighting the Maoris and found themselves out of ammunition and surrounded. The Maori chief called a halt to the fighting and sent a message to the British, saying that they declined to fight them on inferior terms, so they were going to lend the British some of their ammunition. That was gallant to a ridiculous degree, but it was nevertheless a noble impulse. We don't ask of war that it be gallant, but intellectually we cannot afford to be squeamish. I find that where the words, the intellect, the ideas leave off — then the generals take over.

BELL: What is your dominant emotion before a typewriter?

CORWIN: I suppose I begin with a blatant, fundamental, and even atavistic approach to writing, with a sense of indebtedness to those who coined our language, who inflected it and gave it roots and branches and made it blossom. Then, I think, the mixed pleasure and torment of communication takes over, the pleasure to have that language and the tools to employ it, to have some skill in the use of those tools and the productive torment that comes in addressing problems when the communication takes the form of projection of drama or poetry, when it is called upon to oblige its many masters and considerations: truth, felicity, clarity; the avoidance of pomposity; the avoidance of contradiction; a structure that is progressive and not repetitious and says what you want it to say and avoids clichés, that has a rich octane mixture without being too rich because then you get smoke and start choking.

These sometimes come together as a series of nagging little pushes and pulls and tugs and nudges which, when you're not in top form or are worried about any number of things — the next tax payment or the next President — you cannot always make clean-shaven. For example, I try not to mix metaphors but that was one.

BELL: Is it dishonorable to begin writing and know that you will compromise?

CORWIN: I hate compromise, except in the arena of social action, of course, where it is a necessity. But in art, it is an alien force.

Radio Programs

1934   Writer/Director/Producer, *Rhymes and Cadences*, series, WBZ-WBZA.

1937-38 Writer/Director/Producer, *Poetic License*, series, WQXR.

1938   Director/Producer, *Americans at Work*, series, CBS.

Director/Producer, *County Seat*, series written by Milton Geiger, CBS.

Director/Producer, *Columbia Workshop*, (Program: "The Red Badge of Courage"), adapted by Margaret Lewerth, CBS.

Director/Producer, *Columbia Workshop*, (Program: "The Lighthouse Keeper"), CBS.

Director/Producer, *Columbia Workshop*, (Program: "Crosstown Manhattan"), CBS.

Writer/Director/Producer, *Words Without Music*, (Program: "The Plot to Overthrow Christmas"), CBS.

1939   Writer/Director/Producer, *Words Without Music*, (Program: "They Fly Through the Air with the Greatest of Ease"), CBS.

Writer/Director/Producer, *Columbia Workshop,* (Program: "Seems Radio Is Here to Stay"), CBS.

Writer/Director/Producer, *So This Is Radio,* (Programs: "Putting Programs on the Air"; "Twenty Years, the Career of Broadcasting"; "Radio Special Events Department"; "Education via Radio"; "Arrangement and Production of Musical Programs"; "National Association of Broadcasters"), CBS.

Director/Producer, *Columbia Workshop,* (Program: "Journalism in Tennessee"), CBS.

Writer/Director/Producer, *Columbia Workshop,* (Program: "John Brown's Body" — adapted from epic poem by Stephen Vincent Benét), CBS.

Director, *Columbia Workshop,* (Program: radio opera, "Blennerhassett" — text by Phillip Roll, music by Vittorio Giannini), CBS.

1939-40   **Director,** *Pursuit of Happiness* Series, CBS.

1940   **Director/Producer,** *Columbia Workshop,* (Program: "Homecoming" — written by Arthur Laurents), CBS.

Writer/Director/Producer, *Columbia Workshop,* (Program: "My Client Curley" — adapted from story by Lucille Fletcher), CBS.

Writer/Director/Producer, *Forecast,* (Program: "To Tim at Twenty"), CBS.

Writer, *Cavalcade of America,* (Program: "Ann Rutledge" — directed by Homer Fickett), CBS.

1941   **Writer/Director/Producer,** *26 by Corwin,* (Programs: "Radio Primer"; "Log of the R-77"; "The People, Yes"; "Lip Service"; "Appointment"; "The Odyssey of Runyon Jones"; "A Soliloquy to Balance the Budget"; "Daybreak"; "Old Salt"; "Between Americans"; "Ann Rutledge"; "Double Concerto"; "Descent of the Gods"; "Samson"; "Esther"; "Job"; "Mary and the Fairy"; "Anatomy of Sound"; "Fragments from a Lost Cause"; "The Human Angle"; "Good Heavens"; "Wolfeiana"; "Murder in Studio One"; "Descent of the Gods" (repeat); "A Man with a Platform"; "Psalm for a Dark Year"), CBS.

Writer/Director/Producer, *Bill of Rights Special,* (Program: "We Hold These Truths"), a four-network broadcast — CBS, NBC-Red, NBC-Blue, MBS.

1942   **Writer/Director/Producer,** *This Is War!,* (Programs: "America at War"; "It's in the Works"; "The Enemy"; "Concerning Axis Propaganda"; "To the Young"; "Yours Received and Contents Noted"), a four-network broadcast — CBS, NBC-Red, NBC-Blue, MBS.

Writer/Director/Producer, *An American in England,* (Programs: "London by Clipper"; "London to Dover"; "Ration Island"; "Women of Britain"; "The Yanks Are Here"; "An Anglo-American Angle"; "Cromer"; "Home Is Where You Hang Your Helmet"; "Clipper Home"), CBS.

1943   **Writer,** *Cresta Blanca Carnival,* (Program: "A
             Program to Be Opened in a Hundred Years"
             — directed by Berry Kroeger), Mutual
             Broadcasting System.

             Writer/Director/Producer, *America Salutes
             the President's Birthday Party,* (Program: "A
             Moment of the Nation's Time"), CBS.

             Writer/Director/Producer, *Transatlantic Call,*
             (Programs: "New England"; "Washington
             D.C."; "Midwest: Breadbasket and
             Arsenal"), CBS and BBC.

             Writer/Director/Producer, *Passport for
             Adams,* (Programs: "Introduction"; "Tel
             Aviv"; "Moscow"; "Stalingrad"), CBS.

1944   **Writer/Director/Producer,** *Columbia
             Presents Corwin,* (Programs: "Movie Primer";
             "The Long Name None Could Spell"; "The
             Lonesome Train" — written by Millard
             Lampell and Earl Robinson; "Savage
             Encounter"; "The Odyssey of Runyon
             Jones"; "You Can Dream, Inc."; "Untitled";
             "Dorie Got a Medal"; "The Cliché Expert";
             "Cromer"; "New York: A Tapestry for
             Radio"; "Tel Aviv"; "Sandburg"; "Wolfe";
             "Whitman"; "Home for the 4th"; "The Moat
             Farm Murder"; "El Capitan and the
             Corporal"; "A Very Fine Type Girl"; "There
             Will Be Time Later"), CBS.

             Writer/Director/Producer, *Election Eve
             Special,* (Program: "The Roosevelt Special"),
             CBS, NBC-Red, NBC-Blue, Mutual.

1945   **Writer/Director/Producer,** *U.N. San Francisco Conference Special,* (Program: "Word from the People"), CBS.

Writer/Director/Producer, *VE-Day Special,* (Program: "On a Note of Triumph"), CBS.

Writer/Director/Producer, *Columbia Presents Corwin,* (Programs: "Unity Fair"; "Daybreak"; "The Undecided Molecule"; "New York: A Tapestry for Radio"; "A Walk with Nick"; "Savage Encounter"; "L'Affaire Gumpert"), CBS.

Writer/Director/Producer, *VJ-Day Special,* (Program: "14 August"), CBS.

Writer/Director/Producer, *Day of Prayer Special,* (Program: "God and Uranium"), CBS.

Writer/Director/Producer, CBS Promotion Special, (Program: "Stars in the Afternoon"), CBS.

Writer/Director/Producer, Special: *Radio's 25th Anniversary,* (Program: "Seems Radio Is Here to Stay"), CBS.

1947   **Writer/Director/Producer/Narrator,** *One World Flight,* (Programs: "Introduction"; "England"; "France, Denmark, Norway, Sweden"; "Poland"; "Soviet Union"; "Czechoslovakia"; "Italy"; "Egypt, India"; "China"; "Philippines"; "Australia"; "New Zealand"), CBS.

Writer/Director, Special: *Committee for the First Amendment,* (Program: "Hollywood Fights Back" — co-directed by William N. Robson), ABC.

1949   **Writer/Director,** CBS Documentary Unit, (Program: "Citizen of the World" — produced by Werner Michel), CBS.

Writer/Director/Producer, United Nations Radio, (Program: "Could Be"), United Nations Radio.

1950   **Writer/Director/Producer,** *The Pursuit of Peace,* (Program: "Document A/777"), MBS.

Writer/Director/Producer, *United Nations Radio,* (Program: "Fear Itself"), MBS.

1951   **Writer/Director/Producer,** *United Nations Radio,* (Program: "Windows on the World"), United Nations Radio.

1955   **Writer/Director/Producer,** *United Nations Radio,* (Program: "The Charter in the Saucer"), BBC and United Nations Radio.

1969   **Director,** *Ray Bradbury Radio Series,* (Programs: "Forever and the Earth," "The Great Conflagration Up at the Place"), syndication.

1979   **Writer/Director,** *Sears Radio Theatre,* (Program: "The Strange Affliction"), syndication.

1982   **Writer,** *Chicago Radio Theatre* (Program: "The Curse of 589" — directed by Yuri Rasovsky), WMFT, Federation of Community Broadcasters.

1983   **Writer/Director,** *Holiday Series* — produced by Connie Goldman, (Programs: "Memorial Day," "July 4th," "Labor Day," "Columbus Day," "Thanksgiving," "New Year's Day"), National Public Radio.

1991   **Writer,** *Anniversary Special,* (Program: "Bill of Rights: 200" — directed by David Ossman), American Public Radio and NPR.

1993   **Writer/Director,** *The Plot to Overthrow Christmas* — produced by Peggy Webber, broadcast over KNX, KUSC, KPCC, and other stations of APR and NPR.

Filmography

1943   **Writer,** *Forever and a Day*, RKO Pictures. Directed by René Clair, Edmund Goulding, Cedric Hardwicke, Frank Lloyd, Victor Saville, Robert Stevenson, Herbert Wilcox.

1944   **Writer,** *Once Upon a Time*, Columbia Pictures. Directed by Alexander Hall. (Based on "My Client Curley," a radio play by Norman Corwin and Lucille Fletcher.)

1951   **Writer,** *The Blue Veil*, RKO Pictures. Directed by Curtis Bernhardt.

1953   **Writer,** *Scandal at Scourie*, Metro-Goldwyn-Mayer. Directed by Jean Negulesco.

1956   **Writer,** *Lust for Life*, Metro-Goldwyn-Mayer. Directed by Vincente Minnelli.

1960   **Writer,** *The Story of Ruth*, 20th Century-Fox. Directed by Henry Koster.

1962   **Writer,** *Madison Avenue*, 20th Century-Fox. Directed by Bruce Humberstone.

Television Programs

1963   Writer, *F.D.R.*, documentary, episodes #1 and #26, NBC.

1964   **Writer,** *Inside the Movie Kingdom,* documentary, ABC.

1971   **Writer,** *Guest of Honor*, 26 programs, Filmation.

1971-2   **Writer/Director/Co-producer,** *Norman Corwin Presents* (Programs: **writer,** "Two Gods on Prime Time"; **writer,** "You Think You've Got Troubles?"; **writer/director,** "Jefferson's Crush"; **director,** "The First Big Try"; **adapter,** "The Blue Hotel"; **writer/director,** "Crown of Rags"; **writer/director,** "The Discovery"; **writer,** "The Pursuit"; **writer/director,** "Soliloquy for Television"; **writer,** "The Undecided Molecule"; **writer,** "The Moat Farm Murder"; **writer,** "Odyssey in Progress"), Westinghouse Group W and CBC (Canadian Broadcasting Corporation).

1974   **Writer,** *The Plot to Overthrow Christmas*, PBS.

    Writer, *The Court Martial of General Yamashita, Tiger of Malaya* — directed by Stanley Kramer, ABC.

1978   **Writer,** *Network at Fifty,* commemorating
            50th anniversary of CBS — read by Walter
            Cronkite, CBS.

1979   **Writer/Host,** *Academy Leaders,* series, PBS
            (Public Broadcasting System).

Books

1939   *They Fly Through the Air with the Greatest of Ease* (radio play), Vrest Orton, Weston, Vermont.

1940   **The Plot to Overthrow Christmas* (radio play), Peter Pauper Press, Mt. Vernon, New York.

1942   *Thirteen by Corwin* (radio plays), Henry Holt & Co., New York.

We Hold These Truths (radio play), Howell, Soskin, New York.

This Is War! (radio plays), Dodd, Mead & Co., New York.

1944   *More by Corwin* (radio plays), Henry Holt & Co., New York.

1945   *On a Note of Triumph* (radio play), Simon & Schuster, New York.

Med en Ton av Triumf, Förbundets Bökforlag, Stockholm.

1947   *Untitled and Other Plays* (radio plays), Henry Holt & Co., New York.

1952   *Dog in the Sky*, Simon & Schuster, New York.

The Plot to Overthrow Christmas (new version), Henry Holt & Co., New York.

1960   *The Rivalry* (stage play), Dramatists Play Service, New York.

1961	*The World of Carl Sandburg*, Harcourt, Brace & World, New York.
1963	*Overkill and Megalove* (poetry and radio play), World Publishing Co., New York.
1972	**Prayer for the 70s* (poetry), Plantin Press, Los Angeles.
	*Jerusalem Printout, Raintree Press, Bloomington, Indiana.
1978	*Holes in a Stained Glass Window*, Lyle Stuart, Secaucus, New Jersey.
	*Network at Fifty, Invierno Press, Laguna Beach, California.
1981	**A Date with Sandburg*, Santa Susana Press, Northridge, California.
	*Greater Than the Bomb (radio program), Santa Susana Press, Northridge, California.
1983	*Trivializing America*, Lyle Stuart, Secaucus, New Jersey.
1993	Text for *CONartist*, cartoons of Paul Conrad, *Los Angeles Times*, Los Angeles.
1994	*Years of the Electric Ear: Norman Corwin*, interviewed by Douglas Bell; Directors Guild of America Oral History series, Scarecrow Press, Metuchen, New Jersey.
	Norman Corwin's Letters, edited by A.J. Langguth, Barricade Books, New York.

---

*Limited editions

Stage Plays, Musical Productions

1945   **Writer,** Metropolitan Opera, (Program: text of one-act opera, *The Warrior*), music by composer Bernard Rogers, conductor, Max Rudolf; directed by Herbert Graf, Metropolitan Opera House.

1955   **Writer/Director,** *The Golden Door,* a cantata commemorating the tercentenary of Jewish settlement in America; music by Maurice Goldman, who conducted orchestra and chorus; Public Music Hall, Cleveland.

1958   **Writer/Director,** *The Rivalry.* Opened in Vancouver, B.C., toured the U.S., and played on Broadway at the Bijou Theater.

1959   **Writer/Director,** *The World of Carl Sandburg.* Toured the country and played on Broadway at the Henry Miller Theater.

1960   **Writer,** *Yes, Speak Out, Yes,* a cantata for symphony orchestra, chorus and soloists; commissioned by the United Nations and performed in the General Assembly Hall of the UN by the Minneapolis Symphony Orchestra and the Augsburg College Choir under Stanislaw Skrowaczewski and the composer, Cristobal Halffter. Also performed several times in Europe.

1962   **Director,** *The Chinese Wall* by Max Frisch, UCLA Theater Group, UCLA.

1966   **Writer/Director,** *The Hyphen,* commissioned
                  by the University of Utah to dedicate its
                  campus theater, Salt Lake City.

1967   **Writer/Director,** *The Odyssey of Runyon Jones,*
                  musical adaptation of the radio play, with
                  score by Jay Livingston and lyrics by Ray
                  Evans, Valley Music Theatre, Woodland
                  Hills, California.

1973   **Writer,** *Cervantes,* directed by Frank Corsaro,
                  opened in Washington, D.C., and toured the
                  country.

1974   **Writer/Director/Producer,** *Overkill and
                  Megalove,* adapted from the book, presented
                  as a musical play with a score by Josef and
                  Miranda Marais, Desilu Theater, Los
                  Angeles.

1975   **Writer/Director,** *Together Tonight: Jefferson,
                  Hamilton and Burr,* opened at the University
                  of Indiana, Bloomington; toured the country.

Prefaces and Introductions

1947   Preface, *Radio's Best Plays*; Joseph Liss.

1950   Introduction, *Radio Plays For Young People*; Walter Hackett

1986   Introduction, new edition of *Personal History*; Vincent Sheehan

1987   Introduction, *The Musician*; Lyn Murray

1993   Introduction, *For The Sake of Clarity*; Stephen Fritchman

Anthologies

1939   *Best Broadcasts of 1938-1939*; Max Wylie, Whittlesey House, New York.

Columbia Workshop Plays: Fourteen Radio Dramas; Douglas Coulter, Whittlesey House, New York.

1940   *Best Broadcasts of 1939-1940*; Max Wylie, Whittlesey House, New York.

1941   *Best Broadcasts of 1940-1941*; Max Wylie, Whittlesey House, New York.

English Patterns; Roy Johnson, Mabel Bessey, Ginn and Co., Boston.

1942   *This is War!*; H.L. McClinton, Dodd, Mead & Co., New York.

1943   *The Fireside Book of Dog Stories*; Jack Goodman, Simon & Schuster, New York.

War Poems of the United Nations; Joy Davidman, Dial Press, New York.

The Three Readers; Carl Van Doren, Clifton Fadiman, Sinclair Lewis, The Press of the Readers Club, New York.

1944   *Off Mike*; Jerome Lawrence, Duell, Sloan & Pearce, New York.

1945   *This Way to Unity*; Arnold Herrick, Herbert Askwith, Oxford Book Co., New York.

From D-Day Through Victory in Europe, CBS, New York.

1946   *While You Were Gone*; Jack Goodman, Simon & Schuster, New York.

Beyond the Seas; Elizabeth Collette, T.P. Cross, Elmer C. Stauffer, Ginn & Co., Boston.

The Best One-Act Plays of 1945; Margaret Mayorga, Dodd, Mead, New York.

The Saint's Choice of Radio Thrillers, Leslie Charteris, Saint Enterprises, New York.

1947 *American Authors Today*; Whit Burnett, Charles E. Slatkin.

Literature for Our Times; Leonard S. Brown, H.O. Waite, B.P. Atkinson.

Radio's Best Plays; Joseph Liss.

1948 *Words to Live By*, William Nichols, Simon & Schuster, New York.

1950 *Theatre Arts Anthology*; Rosamond Gilder, Hermine Isaacs, R.M. MacGregor, E. Emery, Theatre Arts Books, New York.

Modern One-Act Plays, Griffith and Mersand, Harcourt Brace, New York.

1960 *Lincoln for the Ages*; Ralph G. Newman, Doubleday, Garden City, New York.

1966 *I Have Seen War*; Dorothy Sterling, Hill & Wang, New York.

1970 *The Future Is Now*; William F. Nolan, Sherbourne Press, Los Angeles.

1971 *No Small Plans*; Elizabeth Motherwell, Banff Center, Alberta, Canada.

Maggie; James Bellows, Charles Champlin, Art Seidenbaum, Ward Ritchie Press, Laguna Beach, California.

1973 *The Impact of Film*; Roy Madsen, MacMillan, New York.

1986   *Main Currents in Mass Communications;*
             W.K. Agee, Philip Ault, E. Emery, Harper &
             Row, New York.

1987   *Making America;* Luther S. Luedtke,
             University of North Carolina Press, Chapel
             Hill, North Carolina.

1988   *The North Americans;* James R. Christopher,
             Oxford University Press, New York.

1991   *A Western Harvest;* Frances Ring, John Daniel
             & Co., Santa Barbara, California.

             The Bradbury Chronicles; William F. Nolan,
             M.H. Greenburg, Penguin Books, New York.

1992   *The Ageless Spirit;* Connie Goldman,
             P.L. Berman, Ballantine Books, New York.

             The Broadcast Century; Robert L. Hillard,
             Michael C. Keith, Focal Press, Boston.

Biographical

1975   *This Was Radio* (chapter); Joseph Julian;
Viking Press, New York.

1979   *About Norman Corwin*; text by Ray Bradbury,
photos by Amanda Blanco, Santa Susana
Press.

1985   *Norman Corwin and Radio: The Golden Years*;
R. LeRoy Bannerman; University of Alabama.

13 For Corwin; University of Southern
California.

1986   *Norman Corwin and the Golden Years of Radio:
On a Note of Triumph*, Barricade Books, New
York.

1993   *13 For Corwin*; trade edition, Barricade
Books, New York.

---

*Limited edition

Index